# Fourth Workshop on Hybrid Approaches to Translation 2015



Co-located with ACL-IJCNLP 2015

Beijing, China
31 July 2015

ISBN: 978-1-5108-0941-3

**Printed from e-media with permission by:**

Curran Associates, Inc.
57 Morehouse Lane
Red Hook, NY 12571

**Some format issues inherent in the e-media version may also appear in this print version.**



Printed by Curran Associates, Inc. (2015)

For permission requests, please contact the Association for Computational Linguistics at the address below.

Association for Computational Linguistics
209 N. Eighth Street
Stroudsburg, Pennsylvania 18360

Phone: 1-570-476-8006
Fax: 1-570-476-0860

acl@aclweb.org

**Additional copies of this publication are available from:**

Curran Associates, Inc.
57 Morehouse Lane
Red Hook, NY 12571 USA
Phone: 845-758-0400
Fax: 845-758-2634
Email: curran@proceedings.com
Web: www.proceedings.com

ACL-IJCNLP 2015

# The 53rd Annual Meeting of the Association for Computational Linguistics and the 7th International Joint Conference on Natural Language Processing

## Proceedings of the Fourth Workshop on Hybrid Approaches to Translation (HyTra)

July 31, 2015
Beijing, China

# Introduction

Welcome to the Fourth Workshop on Hybrid Approaches to Translation (HyTra-4) held in conjunction with ACL-2015, Beijing !

The workshop series on Hybrid Approaches to Translation aims at providing a communication platform, building a research community and informing research agenda around theoretical and practical issues of Hybrid MT, and specifically – the problems, methodologies, resources and theoretical ideas which originate outside the mainstream MT paradigm, but have potential to enhance the quality of state-of-the-art MT systems. The workshop series fills in a gap in the current paradigm allowing researchers to explore new pathways of bringing together a diverse range of technologies, methods and tools into MT domain.

The current Fourth Workshop on Hybrid Approaches to Translation - HyTra-4 - builds on a successful series of past events held in conjunction with international conferences (up to this year all of them so far took place in Europe):

HyTra-1 was held (together with the ESIRMT workshop) as a joint 2-day workshop at EACL 2012, Avignon, France: http://www-lium.univ-lemans.fr/esirmt-hytra/

HyTra-2 was a 1-day workshop at ACL 2013, Sophia, Bulgaria: http://hytra.barcelonamedia.org/hytra 2013/

HyTra-3 was a 1-day workshop at the EACL 2014, Gothenburg, Sweden. This workshop for the first time included an Industry Session – with invited talks of representatives from several companies, such as BMMT, SDL, Systran, Tilde, Lingenio company representatives, which highlighted an emerging industrial uptake of the Hybrid MT field by major developers of industrial MT systems: http://parles.upf.edu/llocs/plambert/hytra/hytra2014/

HyTra workshops have attracted a good number of submissions and participants each time, and included invited talks, full papers, and poster sessions. The invited speakers were Philipp Koehn, Hermann Ney, Will Lewis and Chris Quirk, Hans Uszkoreit and Joakim Nivre. The range of topics covered addresses all the areas of linguistic analysis relevant to MT, such as morphology, syntax, discourse, named entity recognition, etc., and a range of underlying MT architectures – statistical and rule-based. The workshops allow sufficient time for panel discussions which take form of exploratory brainstorming sessions and address further pathways of the development and integration of the hybrid MT technologies.

For the HyTra-4 workshop we have accepted 9 papers, which appear in this volume. The workshop hosts the invited talk by Prof. Dr. Hinrich Schuetze, the Chair of Computational Linguistics and the Director of the Center for Information and Language Processing of the Ludwig Maximilian University of Munich, Germany. HyTra-4 also includes the Industry Session, which brings together academic and industrial researchers and practitioners, and is now becoming a traditional part of the workshop.

We hope HyTra-4 will become a successful continuation of the HyTra workshop series and will result in interesting discussions, ideas and collaborations.

Bogdan Babych, University of Leeds
Kurt Eberle, Lingenio GmbH, Heidelberg
Patrik Lambert, Pompeu Fabra University, Barcelona
Reinhard Rapp, University of Mainz
Rafael E. Banchs, Institute for Infocomm Research, Singapore
Marta R. Costa-jussà, Instituto Politécnico Nacional, Mexico

**Organizers:**

Bogdan Babych, University of Leeds
Kurt Eberle, Lingenio GmbH, Heidelberg
Patrik Lambert, Pompeu Fabra University, Barcelona
Reinhard Rapp, University of Mainz
Rafael E. Banchs, Institute for Infocomm Research, Singapore
Marta R. Costa-jussà, Instituto Politécnico Nacional, Mexico

**Program Committee:**

Ahmet Aker, University of Sheffield, UK
Bogdan Babych, University of Leeds, UK
Rafael E. Banchs, Institute for Infocomm Research, Singapore
Alexey Baytin, Yandex, Moscow, Russia
Núria Bel, Universitat Pompeu Fabra, Barcelona, Spain
Anja Belz, University of Brighton, UK
Pierrette Bouillon, ISSCO/TIM/ETI, University of Geneva, Switzerland
Michael Carl, Copenhagen Business School, Denmark
Marta R. Costa-jussà, Instituto Politécnico Nacional, Mexico
Oliver Culo, University of Mainz, Germany
Kurt Eberle, Lingenio GmbH, Heidelberg, Germany
Andreas Eisele, DGT (European Commission), Luxembourg
Marcello Federico, Fondazione Bruno Kessler, Trento, Italy
Christian Federmann, Microsoft Research, Seattle, USA
Maxim Khalilov, BMMT, Germany
Udo Kruschwitz, University of Essex, UK
Patrik Lambert, Pompeu Fabra University, Barcelona, Spain
Yannick Parmentier, Orleans University, France
Reinhard Rapp, University of Mainz, Germany
Serge Sharoff, University of Leeds, UK
George Tambouratzis, Institute for Language and Speech Processing, Athens, Greece
Jörg Tiedemann, University of Uppsala, Sweden

**Invited Speakers:**

Hinrich Schütze, Ludwig Maximilian University of Munich, Germany
Gerard de Melo, Tsinghua University Beijing, China

**Invited Companies of the Industrial Session:**

Baidu
CCID TransTech
Lingenio GmbH

## Table of Contents

# Workshop Program

**Friday, July 31, 2015**

**9:15–10:30 Introduction and Keynote Speech I**

9:15–9:30 *Welcome and introduction*

9:30–10:30 *Invited talk*
Hinrich Schütze

**10:30–11:00 Coffee Break**

**11:00–12:30 Hybrid MT system design**

11:00–11:15 *Bootstrapping a hybrid deep MT system*
João Silva, João Rodrigues, Luís Gomes and António Branco

11:15–11:30 *Multi-system machine translation using online APIs for English-Latvian*
Matīss Rikters

11:30–11:55 *What a Transfer-Based System Brings to the Combination with PBMT*
Aleš Tamchyna and Ondrej Bojar

11:55–12:20 *Establishing sentential structure via realignments from small parallel corpora*
George Tambouratzis and Vassiliki Pouli

**12:20–14:00 Lunch Break**

**Friday, July 31, 2015 (continued)**

**14:00–15:30 Resources and evaluation of hybrid MT systems**

14:00–14:15 *Passive and Pervasive Use of Bilingual Dictionary in Statistical Machine Translation*
Liling Tan

14:15–14:30 *Automated Simultaneous Interpretation: Hints of a Cognitive Framework for Machine Translation*
Rafael E. Banchs

14:30–14:45 *A fuzzier approach to machine translation evaluation: A pilot study on post-editing productivity and automated metrics in commercial settings*
Carla Parra Escartín and Manuel Arcedillo

14:45–15:10 *A Methodology for Bilingual Lexicon Extraction from Comparable Corpora*
Reinhard Rapp

15:10–15:25 *Ongoing Study for Enhancing Chinese-Spanish Translation with Morphology Strategies*
Marta R. Costa-jussà

**15:30–16:00 Coffee Break**

**16:00–17:00 Keynote Speech II**

16:00–17:00 *Invited talk*
Gerard de Melo

**17:00–18:15 Industry applications and Hybrid MT**

17:00–17:30 *Baidu Translate: Research and Products*
Zhongjun He

17:30–18:00 *On Improving the Human Translation Process by Using MT Technologies under a Cognitive Framework*
CCID Trans Tech

18:00–18:15 *Towards a shared task for shallow semantics-based translation (in an industrial setting)*
Kurt Eberle

**Friday, July 31, 2015 (continued)**

**18:15–18:20 Conclusions**

# Bootstrapping a hybrid deep MT system

**João Silva** and **João Rodrigues** and **Luís Gomes** and **António Branco**
University of Lisbon, NLX—Natural Language and Speech Group
Faculdade de Ciências, Universidade de Lisboa
Edifício C6, Piso 3, Campo Grande, 1749-016 Lisboa, Portugal
{jsilva, joao.rodrigues, luis.gomes, antonio.branco}@di.fc.ul.pt

## Abstract

We present a Portuguese↔English hybrid deep MT system based on an analysis-transfer-synthesis architecture, with transfer being done at the level of deep syntax, a level that already includes a great deal of semantic information. The system received a few months of development, but its performance is already similar to that of baseline phrase-based MT, when evaluated using BLEU, and surpasses the baseline under human qualitative assessment.

## 1 Introduction

Data-driven phrase-based MT has been, for many years, the technique that has achieved the best results in MT, much due to the availability of huge parallel data sets. Requiring such large amounts of training data is a hindrance for languages with fewer resources. Statistical MT (SMT) as an approach, however, may have intrinsic limitations that go beyond that of data availability.

The main weakness of current SMT methods ultimately stems from the limited linguistic abstraction that is employed, which leads to difficulties in correctly handling the translation of certain phenomena, such as getting the correct word order when translating between languages with different typology and in maintaining the semantic cohesion of the translated text.

SMT has attempted to tackle these issues by making use of richer linguistic structure, such as hierarchical methods and tree-to-tree mappings, but these methods have been unable to clearly improve on the phrase-based state-of-the-art.

There is a growing opinion that the previous approaches to SMT may be reaching a performance ceiling and that pushing beyond it will require approaches that are more linguistically informed and that are able to bring semantics into the process.

The classic analysis-transfer-synthesis architecture (the Vauquois triangle) provides a promising foundation onto which such approaches can be built. Underlying this architecture is the rationale that, the deeper the level of representation, the easier transfer becomes since deeper representations abstract away from surface aspects that are specific to a language. At the limit, the representation of the meaning of a sentence, and of all its paraphrases, would be shared among all languages.

This paper reports on our work of building a deep MT system, which translates between Portuguese and English, where transfer is performed at the level of a deep syntactic representation.

Portuguese is a widespread language, with an estimated 220 million speakers, and is the fifth most used language on the Web. Despite this, it is relatively less-resourced in terms of available NLP tools and resources (Branco et al., 2012). In this respect, the current work also allowed us to determine a minimal set of NLP tools required to get a deep MT system running, which helps to assess the feasibility of building such a system for under-resourced languages.

This paper is organized as follows. Section 2 presents the translation pipeline. Section 3 evaluates the system intrinsically by comparing it with a state-of-the-art phrase-based SMT approach, and extrinsically by human assessment in the context of a cross-lingual information retrieval task. Section 4 concludes with some final remarks.

## 2 Translation pipeline

Our pipeline is built upon the Treex system (Popel and Žabokrtský, 2010), a modular NLP framework used mostly for MT and the most recent incarnation of the TectoMT system (Žabokrtský et al., 2008). Treex uses an analysis-transfer-synthesis architecture, with transfer being done at the deep syntactic level, where a Tectogrammatical (Tecto) formal description is used.



*Proceedings of the ACL 2015 Fourth Workshop on Hybrid Approaches to Translation (HyTra)*, pages 1–5,
Beijing, China, July 31, 2015. 

The choice of Treex as the supporting framework was motivated by several reasons.

Firstly, Treex is a tried and tested framework that has been shown to achieve very good results in English to Czech translation, on a par with phrase-based SMT systems (Bojar et al., 2013).

Secondly, Treex uses a modular framework, where functionality is separated into *blocks* (of Perl code) that are triggered at different stages of the processing pipeline. This modularity means that we can easily add blocks that make use of existing Portuguese NLP tools and that handle Portuguese-specific phenomena.

Thirdly, English analysis and English synthesis are already provided in Treex, from the work of Popel and Žabokrtský (2010) with Czech, and should be usable in the our pipeline with only little adjustments.

An overview of each of the steps that form the Vauquois triangle—analysis, transfer and synthesis—follows below.

## 2.1 Analysis

Analysis proceeds in two stages. The first stage is a shallow syntactic analysis that takes us from the surface string to what in the Treex framework is called the a-layer (analytical layer), which is a grammatical dependency graph. The second stage is a deep syntactic analysis that takes us from the a-layer to the t-layer (tectogrammatical layer).

### 2.1.1 Getting the a-layer

We resort to LX-Suite (Branco and Silva, 2006), a set of pre-existing shallow processing tools for Portuguese that include a sentence segmenter, a tokenizer, a POS tagger, a morphological analyser and a dependency parser, all with state-of-the-art performance. Treex blocks were created to call and interface with these tools.

After running the shallow processing tools, the dependency output of the parser is converted into Universal Dependencies (UD, (de Marneffe et al., 2014)). These dependencies are then converted into the a-layer tree (a-tree) in a second step. Both steps are implemented as rule-based Treex blocks.

Taking this two-tiered approach to getting the a-tree—first to UD, then from UD to a-tree—has two benefits: (i) it allows us to partly reuse the existing Treex code for converting UD to a-tree, and (ii) it provides us with a way of converting our dependencies into UD, giving us a de facto standard format that may be useful for other applications.

### 2.1.2 Getting the t-layer

Converting the a-tree into a t-layer tree (t-tree) is done through rule-based Treex blocks that manipulate the tree structure.

The major difference between these two trees is that the a-tree, being surface oriented, has a node for each token in the sentence, while the t-tree, being semantically oriented, includes only content words as nodes. Accordingly, the t-tree has no nodes corresponding to auxiliary words, such as prepositions and subordinating conjunctions, but conversely has nodes that do not correspond to any surface word, such as nodes used for representing pro-dropped pronouns.[1]

## 2.2 Transfer

Transfer is handled by a tree-to-tree maximum entropy translation model (Mareček et al., 2010) working at the deep syntactic level of Tecto trees.

This transfer model assumes that the source and target trees are isomorphic. This limitation is rarely a problem since at the Tecto level, as one would expect from a deep syntactic representation, the source and target trees are often isomorphic.

Since the trees are isomorphic, the model is concerned only with learning mappings between t-tree nodes.

The model was trained over 1.9 million sentences from Europarl (Koehn, 2005). Each pair of parallel sentences, one in English and one in Portuguese, are analyzed by Treex up to the t-layer level, where each pair of trees are fed into the model.

## 2.3 Synthesis

Similarly to what was done in analysis, we create new Treex blocks, but resort to pre-existing tools when possible.

The pre-existing tools, for verbal conjugation and for nominal inflection, are rule-based and are used to handle the generation of surface forms.

The rule-based Treex blocks search for patterns over the trees and are used, for instance, to generate to correct word order, to enforce agreement, and to insert the auxiliary words (such as preposition and subordinating conjunctions) that were collapsed when building the t-tree.

[1] Some nodes are removed, but information is preserved as attributes of other nodes or in the relations between nodes.

**Question** I was typing in something and then a blank page appeared before my text, and I do not know how to remove it

**Answer** Move the mouse cursor to the beginning of the blank page and press the DELETE key as often as needed until the text is in the desired spot.

Figure 1: Question-Answer pair

## 3 Evaluation

This Section reports on both an intrinsic and an extrinsic evaluation, the latter made possible by embedding the system into a helpdesk application that provides technical support through an online chat interface. In this regard, the application can be seen as a Question Answering (QA) system.

Since most user questions address issues that have been dealt with previously, they are matched against a database of prior questions-answer pairs. If a matching question is found, the pre-existing answer is returned, thus avoiding the need for the intervention of a human operator.

The questions and the answers in the database are stored in English (see Figure 1 for an example). An MT component enables cross-lingual usage by automatically translating non-English queries into English prior to searching the database, and by automatically translating the answer from English into the language of the user of the application.

The MT component may then impact the QA application in two ways: (i) when translating the question (PT→EN), and consequently affect the ability of the QA system to retrieve the correct answer; and (ii) when translating the retrieved answer (EN→PT), and consequently affect properties of the translated retrieved answer such as its grammaticality, readability and fluency.

Given the workings of this QA application, we are concerned with evaluating translation in the PT→EN direction, for questions, and in the EN→PT direction, for answers.

The test corpus has been developed in the scope of the QTLeap Project. Each question is paired with an answer, both in English, and each of these question-answer pairs has a corresponding reference pair in Portuguese.[2]

[2]The QTLeap project also involves Basque, Bulgarian, Czech, Dutch, German and Spanish, each being paired with English in the same QA application.

| | questions PT→EN | answers EN→PT |
|---|---|---|
| SMT (Moses) | 0.2265 | 0.1899 |
| Treex pipeline | 0.1208 | 0.1943 |

Table 1: Comparison of BLEU scores

### 3.1 Intrinsic evaluation

The intrinsic evaluation is itself broken down into an automatic and a manual evaluation.

In the automatic evaluation, the standard BLEU metric is used to compare the Treex pipeline against a system built with Moses (Koehn et al., 2007) that represents the state-of-the-art SMT phrase-based approach. Like the transfer module in the translation pipeline, the SMT model is trained over 1.9 million sentences from Europarl.

The test set consists of 1,000 question-answer pairs. The results of the automatic intrinsic evaluation are summarized in Table 1.

BLEU scores are low, though we note that the domain of the test corpus (technical support) is very different from the domain of Europarl. For questions, the BLEU score of the Treex pipeline is fairly worse than the score of Moses. Given the application we envisage, this is to be expected. The translated question is meant to be used as database query, and not for human eyes. As such, we have so far placed relatively little effort in improving the synthesis rules for English, since issues like word order errors, agreement mismatches and missing functional words often do not prevent the query from being successful.

BLEU does not necessarily correlate with human judgments. This points us towards manual evaluation as a better way to measure translation quality. Recall that the translation of the retrieved answer, unlike the translation of questions, is meant to be read by humans. As such, the manual evaluation that follows is done only for answers (EN→PT).

The intrinsic manual evaluation consists of a detailed manual diagnosis of the types of translation errors found. Translation errors are classified in a hierarchy of issues, following the Multidimensional Quality Metrics (MQM) framework (Lommel et al., 2014), with the help of the open-source editor translate5.[3] The classification is done by two annotators. Each annotator analyzed the same 100 answers.

[3]http://www.translate5.net/

| | SMT | Treex |
|---|---|---|
| top-1 | 72.8% | 71.6% |
| top-2 | 84.3% | 83.1% |
| top-3 | 87.8% | 87.2% |

Table 2: Answer retrieval

| better variant | |
|---|---|
| Treex pipeline | 30.8% |
| SMT (Moses) | 13.0% |
| (no difference) | 56.2% |

Table 3: Variant ranking

Almost two-thirds of the errors fall under the top-level category Fluency, with nearly 80% of these being classified as Grammar errors, the MQM category that includes issues such as word order, extra words, missing words, agreement problems, among others. The remaining third of the errors are in the top-level category Accuracy, which covers issues where meaning is not preserved, such as mistranslations of domain-specific terminology.

### 3.2 Extrinsic evaluation

The extrinsic evaluation consists of comparing two variants of the cross-lingual QA application, one using the baseline SMT for translation and another using the Treex translation pipeline.

For a given query, the QA system returns a list of answers, each associated with a confidence score.[4] For each variant, we measure if the correct answer is the first result (top-1) or among the top-2 or top-3 returned results. The summary in Table 2 shows that there is little difference between the variants. The Treex pipeline has a lower BLEU for questions, but this does not negatively impact answer retrieval.

While retrieval using the translated question is working well, the quality and usefulness of the helpdesk application ultimately hinges on the quality of the answer that is presented to the user and whether it is correct and clear enough to help the user solve their technical problem.

To evaluate this, a total of six human evaluators were asked to assess the quality of the translated answer. Their task was, given a reference question-answer pair, to compare both translated answers (anonymized and in random order) with the reference answer and pick the best translation, allowing for ties.

While in most cases there is not a clearly better variant, the output of the Treex pipeline is better than the output of the SMT system in 30.8% of the cases and worse in only 13.0% of the cases, as shown in Table 3. Inter-annotator agreement, as a ratio of matched annotations, was 0.628.

[4]The confidence score is based on several factors, such as lexical similarity and the number of times a given answer was used. In the current study, the QA engine is used as a black box and its details are outside the scope of this paper.

## 4 Conclusion

We have presented a Portuguese↔English hybrid deep MT system that, though still under development, achieves a BLEU score similar to that of a SMT system using the state-of-the-art phrase-based approach and, more importantly, is deemed by human evaluators to produce a text with better quality than the SMT system when embedded as part of a QA application.

The system uses an analysis-transfer-synthesis architecture, with transfer being done at the level of deep syntactic trees. This level is oriented towards semantic information, abstracting away auxiliary words while including nodes that do not correspond to any surface word.

Analysis begins by using a set of pre-existing statistical shallow processing tools for Portuguese to produce a grammatical dependency graph. This level of linguistic annotation can be seen as the minimal requirement for bootstrapping a similar deep MT system for other languages. The final step of analysis is rule-based, converting dependency graph into a deep representation. Following statistical transfer, the generation of the target surface form is also a rule-based process.

Evaluation results are very promising and the analysis-transfer-synthesis approach that is used allows much room for improvement apart from just adding more parallel data.

For instance, ongoing research is working towards enriching the pipeline with additional semantic information by plugging in tools for word sense and named-entity disambiguation into the analysis phase, thus providing the transfer phase with disambiguated terms.

## Acknowledgments

This work was partly funded by the EU project QTLeap (EC/FP7/610516) and the Portuguese project DP4LT (PTDC/EEI-SII/1940/2012).

## References

Ondřej Bojar, Christian Buck, Chris Callison-Burch, Christian Federmann, Barry Haddow, Philipp Koehn, Christof Monz, Matt Post, Radu Soricut, and Lucia Specia. 2013. Findings of the 2013 workshop on statistical machine translation. In *Proceedings of the 8th Workshop on Statistical Machine Translation*, pages 1–44.

António Branco and João Silva. 2006. A suite of shallow processing tools for Portuguese: LX-Suite. In *Proceedings of the 11th European Chapter of the Association for Computational Linguistics*, pages 179–182.

António Branco, Amália Mendes, Sílvia Pereira, Paulo Henriques, Thomas Pellegrini, Hugo Meinedo, Isabel Trancoso, Paulo Quaresma, and Vera Lúcia Strube de Lima. 2012. *A Língua Portuguesa na Era Digital / The Portuguese Language in the Digital Age*. White Paper. Springer. ISBN 978-3-642-29592-8.

Marie-Catherine de Marneffe, Natalia Silveira, Timothy Dozat, Katri Haverinen, Filip Ginter, Joakim Nivre, and Christopher Manning. 2014. Universal Stanford dependencies: A cross-linguistic typology. In *Proceedings of the 9th Language Resources and Evaluation Conference*.

Philipp Koehn, Hieu Hoang, Alexandra Birch, Chris Callison-Burch, Marcello Federico, Nicola Bertoldi, Brooke Cowan, Wade Shen, Christine Moran, Richard Zens, Christopher J. Dyer, Ondřej Bojar, Alexandra Constantin, and Evan Herbst. 2007. Moses: Open source toolkit for statistical machine translation. In *Proceedings of the 45th Annual Meeting of the Association for Computational Linguistics Companion Volume Proceedings of the Demo and Poster Sessions*, pages 177–180.

Philipp Koehn. 2005. Europarl: A parallel corpus for statistical machine translation. In *Proceedings of the Tenth Machine Translation Summit*, pages 79–86.

Arle Richard Lommel, Aljoscha Burchardt, and Hans Uszkoreit. 2014. Multidimensional quality metrics (MQM): A framework for declaring and describing translation quality metrics. *Tradumàtica: tecnologies de la traducció*, 0(12):455–463.

David Mareček, Martin Popel, and Zdeněk Žabokrtský. 2010. Maximum entropy translation model in dependency-based MT framework. In *Proceedings of the Joint 5th Workshop on Statistical Machine Translation and MetricsMATR*, pages 201–206.

Martin Popel and Zdeněk Žabokrtský. 2010. TectoMT: Modular NLP framework. In *Proceedings of the 7th International Conference on Natural Language Processing*, pages 293–304.

Zdeněk Žabokrtský, Jan Ptáček, and Petr Pajas. 2008. TectoMT: Highly modular MT system with tectogrammatics used as transfer layer. In *Proceedings of the Third Workshop on Statistical Machine Translation*, pages 167–170.

# Multi-system machine translation using online APIs for English-Latvian

**Matīss Rikters**
University of Latvia
19 Raina Blvd.,
Riga, Latvia
matiss@lielakeda.lv

## Abstract

This paper describes a hybrid machine translation (HMT) system that employs several online MT system application program interfaces (APIs) forming a Multi-System Machine Translation (MSMT) approach. The goal is to improve the automated translation of English – Latvian texts over each of the individual MT APIs. The selection of the best hypothesis translation is done by calculating the perplexity for each hypothesis. Experiment results show a slight improvement of BLEU score and WER (word error rate).

## 1 Introduction

MSMT is a subset of HMT where multiple MT systems are combined in a single system to complement each other's weaknesses in order to boost the accuracy level of the translations. Other types of HMT include modifying statistical MT (SMT) systems with rule-based MT (RBMT) generated output and generating rules for RBMT systems with the help of SMT [19].

MSMT involves usage of multiple MT systems in parallel and combining their output with the aim to produce better result as for each of the individual systems. It is a relatively new branch of MT and interest from researchers has emerged more widely during the last 10 years. And even now such systems mostly live as experiments in lab environments instead of real, live, functional MT systems. Since no single system can be perfect and different systems have different advantages over others, a good combination must lead towards better overall translations.

There are several recent experiments that use MSMT. Ahsan and Kolachina [1] describe a way of combining SMT and RBMT systems in multiple setups where each one had input from the SMT system added in a different phase of the RBMT system.

Barrault [3] describes a MT system combination method where he combines confusion networks of the best hypotheses from several MT systems into one lattice and uses a language model for decoding the lattice to generate the best hypothesis.

Mellebeek et al. [12] introduce a hybrid MT system that utilised online MT engines for MSMT. They introduce a system that at first attempts to split sentences into smaller parts for easier translation by the means of syntactic analysis, then translate each part with each individual MT system while also providing some context, and finally create the output from the best scored translations of each part (they use three heuristics for selecting the best translation).

Most of the research is done English – Hindi, Arabic – English and English – Spanish language pairs in their experiments. Where it concerns English - Latvian machine translation, no such experiments have been conducted.

This paper presents a first attempt in using an MSMT approach for the under-resourced English-Latvian language pair. Furthermore the first results of this hybrid system are analysed and compared with human evaluation. The experiments described use multiple combinations of outputs from two MT systems and one experiment uses three different MT systems.



*Proceedings of the ACL 2015 Fourth Workshop on Hybrid Approaches to Translation (HyTra)*, pages 6–10,
Beijing, China, July 31, 2015. 

## 2 System description

The main system consists of three major constituents – tokenization of the source text, the acquisition of a translation via online APIs and the selection of the best translation from the candidate hypotheses. A visualized workflow of the system is presented in Figure 1.

Currently the system uses three translation APIs (Google Translate[1], Bing Translator[2] and LetsMT[3]), but it is designed to be flexible and adding more translation APIs has been made simple. Also, it is initially set to translate from English into Latvian, but the source and target languages can also be changed to any language pair supported by the APIs.

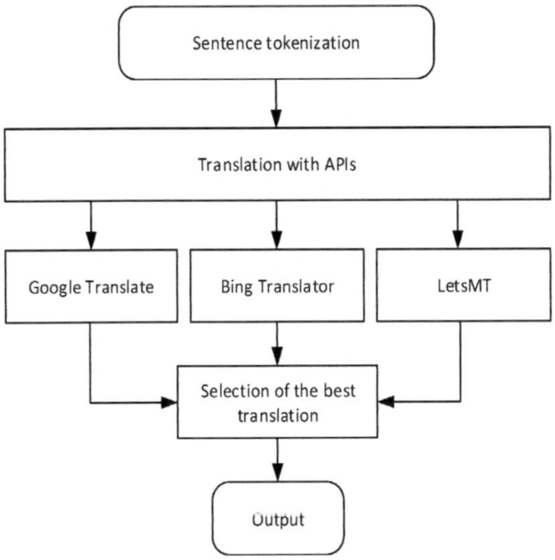


*Figure 1: General workflow of the translation process*

### 2.1 API description

Currently there are three online translation APIs included in the project – Google Translate, Bing Translator and LetsMT. These specific APIs were chosen for their public availability and descriptive documents as well as the wide range of languages that they offer. One of the main criteria when searching for translation APIs was the option to translate from English to Latvian.

### 2.2 Selection of the final translation

The selection of the best translation is done by calculating the perplexity of each hypothesis translation using KenLM [8]. First, a language model (LM) must be created using a preferably large set of training sentences. Then for each machine-translated sentence a perplexity score represents the probability of the specific sequence of words appearing in the training corpus used to create the LM. Sentence perplexity has been proven to correlate with human judgments close to the BLEU score and is a good evaluation method for MT without reference translations [7]. It has been also used in other previous attempts of MSMT to score output from different MT engines as mentioned by Callison-Burch et al. [4] and Akiba et al. [2].

KenLM calculates probabilities based on the observed entry with longest matching history $w_f^n$:

$$p\left(w_n \mid w_1^{n-1}\right) = p\left(w_n \mid w_f^{n-1}\right) \prod_{i=1}^{f-1} b\left(w_i^{n-1}\right)$$

where the probability $p\left(w_n \mid w_f^{n-1}\right)$ and backoff penalties $b\left(w_i^{n-1}\right)$ are given by an already-estimated language model. Perplexity is then calculated using this probability:

$$b^{-\frac{1}{N}\sum_{i=1}^{N}\log_b q(x_i)}$$

where given an unknown probability distribution $p$ and a proposed probability model $q$, it is evaluated by determining how well it predicts a separate test sample $x_1, x_2... x_N$ drawn from $p$.

## 3 System usage

The source code with working examples and sample data has been made open source and is available on GitHub[4]. To run the basic setup a Linux system is required with PHP and cURL installed. Before running, the user needs to edit the MSHT.php file and add his Google Translate, Bing Translator and LetsMT credentials as well as specify source and target languages (the defaults are set for English – Latvian).

The data required for an experiment is a source language text as a plain text file and a language model. The LM can be generated via KenLM using a large monolingual training corpus. The LM should be converted to binary format for more efficient usage.

[1] Google Translate API - https://cloud.google.com/translate/

[2] Bing Translator Control - http://www.bing.com/dev/en-us/translator

[3] LetsMT! Open Translation API - https://www.letsmt.eu/Integration.aspx

[4] Multi-System-Hybrid-Translator - https://github.com/M4t1ss/Multi-System-Hybrid-Translator

## 4 Experiments

The first experiments were conducted on the English – Latvian part of the JRC Acquis corpus version 2.2 [18] from which both the language model and the test data were retrieved. The test data contained 1581 randomly selected sentences. The language model was created using KenLM with order 5.

Translations were obtained from each API individually, combining each two APIs and lastly combining all three APIs. Thereby forming 7 different variants of translations. Google Translate and Bing Translator APIs were used with the default configuration and the LetsMT API used the configuration of TB2013 EN-LV v03[5].

Evaluation on each of the seven outputs was done with three scoring methods – BLEU [13], TER (translation edit rate) [16] and WER [9]. The resulting translations were inspected with a modified iBLEU tool [11] that allowed to determine which system from the hybrid setups was chosen to get the specific translation for each sentence.

The results of the first translation experiment are summarized in Table 2. Surprisingly all hybrid systems that include the LetsMT API produce lower results than the baseline LetsMT system. However the combination of Google Translate and Bing Translator shows improvements in BLEU score and WER compared to each of the baseline systems.

The table also shows the percentage of translations from each API for the hybrid systems. Although according to scores the LetsMT system was by far better than the other two, it seems that the language model was reluctant to favor its translations.

Since the systems themselves are more of a general domain and the first test was conducted on a legal domain corpus, a second experiment was conducted on a smaller data set containing 512 sentences of a general domain [15]. In this experiment only the BLEU score was calculated as it is shown in Table 1.

| System | BLEU |
|---|---|
| Google Translate | 24.73 |
| Bing Translator | 22.07 |
| LetsMT | 32.01 |
| Hybrid Google + Bing | 23.75 |
| Hybrid Google + LetsMT | 28.94 |
| Hybrid LetsMT + Bing | 27.44 |
| Hybrid Google + Bing + LetsMT | 26.74 |

*Table 1: Second experiment results*

| System | BLEU | TER | WER | Translations selected | | | |
|---|---|---|---|---|---|---|---|
| | | | | Google | Bing | LetsMT | Equal |
| Google Translate | 16.92 | 47.68 | 58.55 | 100 % | - | - | - |
| Bing Translator | 17.16 | 49.66 | 58.40 | - | 100 % | - | - |
| LetsMT | 28.27 | 36.19 | 42.89 | - | - | 100 % | - |
| Hybrid Google + Bing | 17.28 | 48.30 | 58.15 | 50.09 % | 45.03 % | - | 4.88 % |
| Hybrid Google + LetsMT | 22.89 | 41.38 | 50.31 | 46.17 % | - | 48.39 % | 5.44 % |
| Hybrid LetsMT + Bing | 22.83 | 42.92 | 50.62 | - | 45.35 % | 49.84 % | 4.81 % |
| Hybrid Google + Bing + LetsMT | 21.08 | 44.12 | 52.99 | 28.93 % | 34.31 % | 33.98 % | 2.78 % |

*Table 2: First experiment results*

| System | User 1 | User 2 | User 3 | User 4 | User 5 | AVG user | Hybrid | BLEU |
|---|---|---|---|---|---|---|---|---|
| **Bing** | 21,88% | 53,13% | 28,13% | 25,00% | 31,25% | 31,88% | 28,93% | 16.92 |
| **Google** | 28,13% | 25,00% | 25,00% | 28,13% | 46,88% | 30,63% | 34,31% | 17.16 |
| **LetsMT** | 50,00% | 21,88% | 46,88% | 46,88% | 21,88% | 37,50% | 33,98% | 28.27 |

*Table 3: Native speaker evaluation results*

[5] https://www.letsmt.eu/TranslateText.aspx?id=smt-e3080087-866f-498b-977d-63ea391ba61e

## 5 Human evaluation

A random 2% (32 sentences) of the translations from the first experiment were given to five native Latvian speakers with an instruction to choose the best translation (just like the hybrid system should). The results are shown in Table 3. Comparing the evaluation results to the BLEU scores and the selections made by the hybrid MT a tendency towards the LetsMT translation can be observed among the user ratings and BLEU score that is not visible from the selection of the hybrid method.

## 6 Conclusion

This short paper described a machine translation system combination approach using public online MT system APIs. The main focus was to gather and utilize only the publically available APIs that support translation for the under-resourced English-Latvian language pair.

One of the test cases showed an improvement in BLEU score and WER over the best baseline.

In all hybrid systems that included the LetsMT API a decline in overall translation quality was observed. This can be explained by scale of the engines - the Bing and Google systems are more general, designed for many language pairs, whereas the MT system in LetsMT was specifically optimized for English – Latvian translations. This problem could potentially be resolved by creating a language model using a larger training corpus and a higher order for more precision.

## 7 Future work

The described system currently is only at the beginning of its lifecycle and further improvements are planned ahead. There are several methods that could improve the current system combination approach. One way is the application of other possible methods for selection of the best hypothesis.

For instance – the QuEst framework [17] can be used to extract various linguistic features for each sentence in the training corpora. Afterwards using the features along with a quality rating for each sentence a machine learning algorithm can train a model for predicting translation quality. The resulting model can then evaluate each candidate translation in a multi-system setup instead of perplexity.

Another path for hypothesis selection is the creation of a confusion network as described by Rosti, et al. [14]. This can be done with tools from either the Hidden Markov Toolkit[6] or the NIST Scoring Toolkit[7].

It would also be worth looking into any other forms of evaluating translations that do not require reference translations or MT quality estimation. For instance an evaluation using n-gram co-occurrence statistics as mentioned by Doddington [6] and Lin et al. [10] or quality estimation using tree kernels introduced by Cohn et al. [5].


## Acknowledgements

This research work was supported by the research project "Optimization methods of large scale statistical models for innovative machine translation technologies", project financed by The State Education Development Agency (Latvia) and European Regional Development Fund, contract No. 2013/0038/2DP/2.1.1.1.0/13/APIA/ VI-AA/029. The author would also like to thank Inguna Skadiņa for advices and contributions, and the anonymous reviewers for their comments and suggestions.


## Reference


[1] Ahsan, A., and P. Kolachina. "Coupling Statistical Machine Translation with Rule-based Transfer and Generation, AMTA-The Ninth Conference of the Association for Machine Translation in the Americas." Denver, Colorado (2010).

[2] Akiba, Yasuhiro, Taro Watanabe, and Eiichiro Sumita. "Using language and translation models to select the best among outputs from multiple MT systems." Proceedings of the 19th international conference on Computational linguistics-Volume 1. Association for Computational Linguistics, 2002.

[3] Barrault, Loïc. "MANY: Open source machine translation system combination." The Prague Bulletin of Mathematical Linguistics 93 (2010): 147-155.

[4] Callison-Burch, Chris, and Raymond S. Flournoy. "A program for automatically selecting the best output from multiple machine translation


[6] HTK Speech Recognition Toolkit - http://htk.eng.cam.ac.uk/

[7] NIST Scoring Toolkit Version 0.1 - http://www1.icsi.berkeley.edu/Speech/docs/sctk-1.2/sctk.htm

engines." Proceedings of the Machine Translation Summit VIII. 2001.

[5] Cohn, Trevor, and Lucia Specia. "Modelling Annotator Bias with Multi-task Gaussian Processes: An Application to Machine Translation Quality Estimation." ACL (1). 2013.

[6] Doddington, George. "Automatic evaluation of machine translation quality using n-gram co-occurrence statistics." Proceedings of the second international conference on Human Language Technology Research. Morgan Kaufmann Publishers Inc., 2002.

[7] Gamon, Michael, Anthony Aue, and Martine Smets. "Sentence-level MT evaluation without reference translations: Beyond language modeling." Proceedings of EAMT. 2005.

[8] Heafield, Kenneth. "KenLM: Faster and smaller language model queries." Proceedings of the Sixth Workshop on Statistical Machine Translation. Association for Computational Linguistics, 2011.

[9] Klakow, Dietrich, and Jochen Peters. "Testing the correlation of word error rate and perplexity." Speech Communication 38.1 (2002): 19-28.

[10] Lin, Chin-Yew, and Eduard Hovy. "Automatic evaluation of summaries using n-gram co-occurrence statistics." Proceedings of the 2003 Conference of the North American Chapter of the Association for Computational Linguistics on Human Language Technology-Volume 1. Association for Computational Linguistics, 2003.

[11] Madnani, Nitin. "iBLEU: Interactively debugging and scoring statistical machine translation systems." Semantic Computing (ICSC), 2011 Fifth IEEE International Conference on. IEEE, 2011.

[12] Mellebeek, Bart, et al. "Multi-engine machine translation by recursive sentence decomposition." (2006).

[13] Papineni, Kishore, et al. "BLEU: a method for automatic evaluation of machine translation." Proceedings of the 40th annual meeting on association for computational linguistics. Association for Computational Linguistics, 2002.

[14] Rosti, Antti-Veikko I., et al. "Combining Outputs from Multiple Machine Translation Systems." HLT-NAACL. 2007.

[15] Skadiņa, Inguna, et al. "A Collection of Comparable Corpora for Under-resourced Languages." Proceedings of the Fourth International Conference Baltic HLT 2010. 2010.

[16] Snover, Matthew, et al. "A study of translation edit rate with targeted human annotation." Proceedings of association for machine translation in the Americas. 2006.

[17] Specia, Lucia, et al. "QuEst-A translation quality estimation framework." ACL (Conference System Demonstrations). 2013.

[18] Steinberger, Ralf, et al. "The JRC-Acquis: A multilingual aligned parallel corpus with 20+ languages." arXiv preprint cs/0609058 (2006).

[19] Thurmair, Gregor. "Comparingdifferentarchitecturesof hybridMachineTranslationsystems." (2009).

# What a Transfer-Based System Brings to the Combination with PBMT

**Aleš Tamchyna** and **Ondřej Bojar**
Charles University in Prague, Faculty of Mathematics and Physics
Institute of Formal and Applied Linguistics
Malostranské náměstí 25, Prague, Czech Republic
surname@ufal.mff.cuni.cz

## Abstract

We present a thorough analysis of a combination of a statistical and a transfer-based system for English→Czech translation, Moses and TectoMT. We describe several techniques for inspecting such a system combination which are based both on automatic and manual evaluation. While TectoMT often produces bad translations, Moses is still able to select the good parts of them. In many cases, TectoMT provides useful novel translations which are otherwise simply unavailable to the statistical component, despite the very large training data. Our analyses confirm the expected behaviour that TectoMT helps with preserving grammatical agreements and valency requirements, but that it also improves a very diverse set of other phenomena. Interestingly, including the outputs of the transfer-based system in the phrase-based search seems to have a positive effect on the search space. Overall, we find that the components of this combination are complementary and the final system produces significantly better translations than either component by itself.

## 1 Introduction

Chimera (Bojar et al., 2013b; Tamchyna et al., 2014) is a hybrid English-to-Czech MT system which has repeatedly won in the WMT shared translation task (Bojar et al., 2013a; Bojar et al., 2014). It combines a statistical phrase-based system (Moses, in a factored setting), a deep-transfer hybrid system TectoMT (Popel and Žabokrtský, 2010) and a rule-based post-editing tool Depfix (Rosa et al., 2012).

Empirical results show that each of the components contributes significantly to the translation quality, together setting the state of the art for English→Czech translation. While the effects of Depfix have been thoroughly analyzed in Bojar et al. (2013b), the interplay between the two translation systems (Moses and TectoMT) has not been examined so far.

In this paper, we show how exactly a deep transfer-based system helps in statistical MT. We believe that our findings are not limited to our exact setting but rather provide a general picture that applies also to other hybrid MT systems and other translation pairs with rich target-side morphology.

The paper is organized as follows: Section 2 briefly describes the architecture of Chimera and summarizes its results in the WMT shared tasks. In Section 3, we analyze what the individual components of Chimera contribute to translation quality. Section 4 describes how the components complement each other Section 5 outlines some of the problems still present in Chimera and Section 6 concludes the paper.

## 2 Chimera Overview

Chimera is a system combination of a phrase-based Moses system (Koehn et al., 2007) with TectoMT (Popel and Žabokrtský, 2010), finally processed with Depfix (Rosa et al., 2012), an automatic correction of morphological and some semantic errors (reversed negation). Chimera thus does not quite fit in the classification of hybrid MT systems suggested by Costa-jussà and Fonollosa (2015).

Figure 1 provides a graphical summary of the simple system combination technique dubbed "poor man's", as introduced by Bojar et al. (2013b). The system combination does not need any dedicated tool, e.g. those by Matusov et al. (2008), Barrault (2010), or Heafield and Lavie (2010). Instead, it directly includes the output of the transfer-based system into the main phrase-based search.



*Proceedings of the ACL 2015 Fourth Workshop on Hybrid Approaches to Translation (HyTra)*, pages 11–20,
Beijing, China, July 31, 2015. 

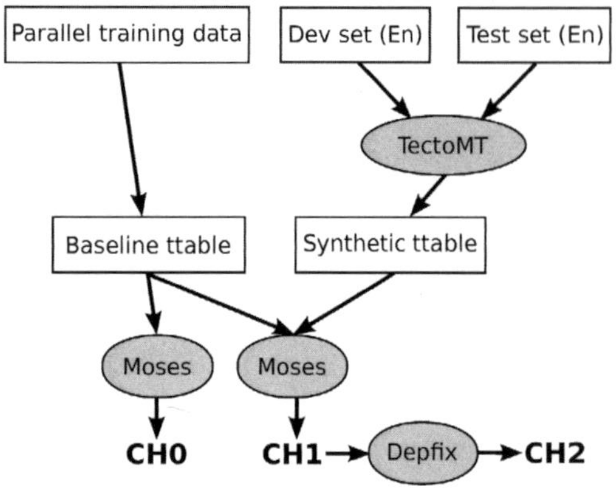


Figure 1: "Poor man's system combination".

At its core, Chimera is a (factored) Moses system with two phrase tables. The first is a standard phrase table extracted from English-Czech parallel data. The second phrase table is tailored to the input data and comes from a synthetic parallel corpus provided by TectoMT: the source sides of the dev *and* test sets are first translated with CU-TECTOMT. Following the standardard word alignment on the source side and the translation, phrases are extracted from this synthetic corpus and added as a separate phrase table to the combined system (CH1). The relative importance of this phrase table is estimated in standard MERT (Och, 2003).

The final translation of the test set is produced by Moses (enriched with this additional phrase table) and additionally post-processed by Depfix.

Note that all components of this combination have direct access to the source side which prevents the cumulation of errors.

For brevity, we will use the following names: CH0 to denote the plain Moses, CH1 to denote the Moses combining the two phrase tables (one from CH0 and one from CU-TECTOMT), and CH2 to denote the final CHIMERA.

In this paper, we focus on the first two components, leaving CH2 aside. The rest of this section summarizes Chimera's results in the last three years of WMT translation task and adds two technical details: language models used in 2015 and the effects of the default low phrase table limit.

### 2.1 Chimera and its Components in WMT

Table 1 shows the official BLEU scores and the results of manual evaluation (ranking) in the last three years of WMT. It illustrates the complementary value of each component in Chimera.

| | System | BLEU | TER | Manual |
|---|---|---|---|---|
| WMT13 | CH2 | 20.0 | **0.693** | **0.664** |
| | CH1 | **20.1** | 0.696 | 0.637 |
| | CH0 | 19.5 | 0.713 | – |
| | GOOGLE TRANSLATE | 18.9 | 0.720 | 0.618 |
| | CU-TECTOMT | 14.7 | 0.741 | 0.455 |
| WMT14 | CH2 | 21.1 | 0.670 | **0.373** |
| | UEDIN-UNCONSTR. | **21.6** | **0.667** | 0.357 |
| | CH1 | 20.9 | 0.674 | 0.333 |
| | GOOGLE TRANSLATE | 20.2 | 0.687 | 0.168 |
| | CU-TECTOMT | 15.2 | 0.716 | -0.177 |
| WMT15 | CH2 | **18.8** | **0.715** | pending |
| | CH1 | 18.7 | 0.717 | – |
| | NEURALMTPRIMARY | 18.3 | 0.719 | pending |
| | CH0 | 17.6 | 0.730 | – |
| | GOOGLE TRANSLATE | 16.4 | 0.750 | pending |
| | CU-TECTOMT | 13.4 | 0.763 | pending |

Table 1: Automatic scores and results of manual ranking (where available) in the last three years of WMT. BLEU (cased) and TER from `matrix.statmt.org`. The top other system and GOOGLE TRANSLATE reported for reference.

| LM ID | factor | order | # tokens |
|---|---|---|---|
| long | stc | 7 | 685M |
| big | stc | 4 | 3903M |
| morph | tag | 10 | 817M |
| longm | tag | 15 | 817M |

Table 2: Overview of LMs used in Chimera.

TectoMT by itself does not perform well compared to other systems in the task, it consistently achieves low BLEU scores and manual ranking. Moses by itself (CH0) achieves quite a high BLEU score but still significantly lower than CH1 (combination of the "poor" TectoMT and plain Moses). Depfix seems to make almost no difference in the automatic scores (once it even slightly worsened the BLEU score) but CH2 has been consistently significantly better in manual evaluation. In 2014, Chimera would have lost to Edinburgh's submission if it were not for Depfix.

An illustration of the complementary utility is given in Table 3. Both CH0 and CU-TECTOMT produce translations with major errors. CH1 is able to pick the best of both and produce a grammatical and adequate output, very similar to the reference translation. CH1 can also produce words which were not present in either output.

### 2.2 Language Models

In 2015, CHIMERA in all its stages used four language models (LMs), as summarized in Table 2.

Two of the language models ("big" and "long") are trained on surface forms ("stc" refers to *su-*

| | |
|---|---|
| **source** | the living zone with the dining room and kitchen section in the household of the young couple . |
| **reference** | obývací zóna s jídelní a kuchyňskou částí v domácnosti mladého páru .<br>*living zone with dining and kitchen section in household young*$_{gen}$ *couple*$_{gen}$ . |
| CH0 | obývací zóna s jídelnou a kuchyní **v sekci** domácnosti **mladý pár** .<br>*living zone with dining_room and kitchen* **in section** *household*$_{gen}$ **young**$_{nom}$ **couple**$_{nom}$ . |
| CU-TECTOMT | **živá** zóna **pokoje** s jídelnou a s kuchyňským oddílem v domácnosti mladého páru .<br>**alive** *zone* **room**$_{gen}$ *with dining_room and with kitchen section in household young*$_{gen}$ *couple*$_{gen}$ . |
| CH1 | obývací prostor s jídelnou a kuchyní v domácnosti mladého páru .<br>*living space with dining_room and kitchen in household young*$_{gen}$ *couple*$_{gen}$ . |

Table 3: Example of translations by various stages of Chimera. Errors are in bold, glosses are in italics.

| system | table limit | | BLEU |
|---|---|---|---|
| | CH0 | TectoMT | |
| CH1 | 100 | 20 | 24.23±0.10 |
| | 100 | 100 | 24.16±0.07 |
| | 20 | 20 | 24.00±0.04 |
| | 20 | 100 | 23.96±0.03 |
| CH0 | 100 | – | 22.57±0.16 |
| | 20 | – | 22.46±0.15 |

Table 4: Impact of phrase table limit for phrase tables coming from the parallel data (the column "CH0") and from TectoMT.

| CU-TECTOMT | CH0 | CH1 | Tokens | Types | | | |
|---|---|---|---|---|---|---|---|
| | | | 1gr | 1gr | 2gr | 3gr | 4gr |
| ✓ | ✓ | ✓ | 44.7% | 41.6% | 15.1% | 6.5% | 3.0% |
| - | - | - | 32.9% | 35.0% | 63.0% | 77.5% | 85.8% |
| - | ✓ | ✓ | 8.6% | 8.8% | 9.3% | 7.2% | 5.1% |
| ✓ | - | ✓ | 4.5% | 4.8% | 3.8% | 2.5% | 1.5% |
| - | ✓ | - | 3.6% | 3.8% | 3.5% | 2.5% | 1.8% |
| ✓ | - | - | 3.5% | 3.7% | 2.9% | 1.9% | 1.2% |
| - | - | ✓ | 1.4% | 1.4% | 1.9% | 1.8% | 1.5% |
| ✓ | ✓ | - | 0.8% | 0.8% | 0.4% | 0.2% | 0.1% |
| Total (100 %) | | | 60584 | 56298 | 57284 | 54536 | 51567 |

Table 5: Which component provided various $n$-grams needed by the reference?

*pervised truecasing*, where the casing is determined by the lemmatizer) and two on morphological tags. Since tags are much less sparse than word forms, we can use a higher LM order. The new "long morphological", dubbed "longm", was aimed at capturing common sentential morphosyntactic patterns.

### 2.3 Phrase Table Limit

Until recently we did not pay much attention to the maximum number of different translation options considered per source phrase (the parameter `table-limit`), assuming that the good phrase pairs are scored high and will be present in the list.

This year, we set `table-limit` to 100 instead of the default 20 and found that while it indeed made little or no difference in CH0, it affected the system combination in CH1. It is known that multiple phrase tables clutter the search space with different derivations of the same output (Bojar and Tamchyna, 2011), demanding a relaxation of pruning during the search (e.g. `stack-limit` or the various limits of cube pruning). From this point of view, increasing the `table-limit` actually makes the situation worse by bringing in more options. We leave the search pruning limits at their default values, increase only the `table-limit`, and yet observe a gain.

Table 4 shows the average testset BLEU score (incl. the standard deviation) obtained in three independent runs of MERT when setting the `table-limit` to 20 or 100 for one or both phrase tables. Multeval (Clark et al., 2011) confirmed that the difference between 20 and 100 for both tables of CH1 (i.e. 24.00 vs. 24.16) is significant while the difference for the system CH0 is not. A part of this effect has to be attributed to the lower variance of CH1 MERT runs, indicating that the TectoMT phrase table somehow stabilizes the search. This could be due to the longer phrases from TectoMT, see Section 3.1. The results also suggest that keeping the default limit for the TectoMT phrase table would have been an even better choice – perhaps because low scoring phrases from TectoMT are indeed mostly bad while the relaxed CH0 `table-limit` ensures that the necessary morphological variants of words are considered at all.

## 3 Contribution of Individual Components

Table 5 breaks $n$-grams from the reference of WMT14 test set into classes depending on by which Chimera components they were produced. The first column considers unigram tokens, the subsequent columns report $n$-gram types.

We see that 44.7 % of unigram tokens needed by the reference were available in all (✓✓✓) components, i.e. CU-TECTOMT, CH0, and surviving in the combination CH1. On the other hand 32.9 %

| | | CU-TECTOMT | CHO | **both** | **total** |
|---|---|---|---|---|---|
| **phrase tokens** | count | 3606 | 10033 | 18322 | 31961 |
| | avg. len. | 3.68 | 2.47 | 1.56 | 2.08 |
| **phrase types** | count | 3503 | 9400 | 8203 | 21106 |
| | avg. len. | 3.73 | 2.52 | 2.07 | 2.54 |

Table 6: Phrase counts and average phrase pairs divided by their source.

tokens were not available in any of these single-best outputs. For Czech as a morphologically rich target language, it is a common fact that a large portion of the output is not confirmed by the reference (and vice versa) despite not containing any errors (Bojar et al., 2010).

The poor man's system combination method is essentially phrase-based, so it is not surprising that there are about twice as many unigrams that come from CHO than from CU-TECTOMT, see 8.6 vs 4.5 %. This bias towards PBMT gets more pronounced with longer n-grams (5.1 vs 1.5 % for 4-grams). The number of $n$-grams needed by the reference and coming from either of the individual systems but not appearing in the combination (-✓- and ✓--) is comparable, around 3.5 % of unigrams.

It is good news that we gain ~1.5 % of $n$-grams as a side-effect: neither of the systems suggested them on its own but they appeared in the combination (--✓). Note that we see this positive effect also for unigrams, suggesting that our "poor man's" system combination could in principle outperform more advanced techniques. The output of the secondary system(s) can help the main search to come up with better translation options.

In the following, we refine the analysis of contributions of the individual components by finding *where* they apply and *what* they improve.

### 3.1 Sources of Used Phrase Pairs

In a separate analysis, we look at the translation of the WMT13 test set and the phrases used to produce it. Table 6 shows both phrase counts and average (source) phrase lengths (in words) broken down according to the phrase source. The test set was translated using 31961 phrases in total ("phrase tokens"), 21106 unique phrase pairs were used ("phrase types"). Many phrase pairs were available in both phrase tables.

The TectoMT phrase table provided 11706 phrase types in total, 3503 of these were unique, i.e. not present in the phrase table extracted from the parallel data. (See Section 4.1 below for the reachability of such phrases on the WMT14 test set.) Given the total number of phrase types, this is a small minority (roughly 17 %), however these phrases correspond directly to our test set and the benefit is visible right away: the average phrase length of these unique phrases is much higher (3.73) which allows the decoder to cover longer parts of the input by a single phrase. We believe that such phrases help preserve local (morphological) agreement and overall consistency of the translation.[1]

As expected, the average length of the shared phrase pairs (present in both phrase tables) is short and this is even more prominent when we look at tokens (phrase occurrences) where the average length is only 1.56. Again, phrase tokens provided by TectoMT are significantly longer, 3.68 words on average.

### 3.2 Correctness of Phrases from CHO vs. CU-TECTOMT

Phrase-based MT relies on phrase pairs automatically extracted from parallel data. This process uses imperfect word alignment and several heuristics and therefore, phrase tables often contain spurious translation pairs. Moreover, phrases extracted from synthetic data (where the target side was produced automatically) can contain errors made by the translation system.

In this analysis, our basic aim was to compare the quality of phrases extracted from parallel data and phrases provided by TectoMT. This analysis was done manually on data samples by two independent annotators. We looked at the percentage of such bad phrase pairs in two settings:

- phrase pairs contained in the phrase table
- phrase pairs used in the 1-best translation

We can assume that most of the noisy phrase pairs in the phrase tables are never used in practice (they are improbable according to the data or they apply to some very uncommon source phrase). That is why we also looked at phrase pairs *actually used* in producing the 1-best translation of the WMT 13 test set.

For each of the two settings, we took a random sample of 100 phrase pairs from each source of

[1]Outputs of TectoMT tend to be grammatical sentences. The surface realization is generated from a deep-syntactic representation using a sequence of steps which preserve the imposed agreement constraints.

data and had two annotators evaluate them. The basic annotation instruction was: "Mark a phrase pair as correct if you can imagine at least some context where it could provide a valid translation." In other words, we are checking if a phrase pair introduces an error already on its own.

| | | OK | Bad | Unsure | IAA |
|---|---|---|---|---|---|
| **ttable** | CH0 | 76.0% | 17.5% | 6.5% | 78.0 |
| | CU-TECTOMT | 66.3% | 26.3% | 7.4% | 83.0 |
| **used** | CH0 | 89.0% | 7.5% | 3.5% | 94.0 |
| | CU-TECTOMT | 87.5% | 9.0% | 3.5% | 87.0 |

Table 7: Correctness of phrases in CHIMERA's phrase tables.

Table 7 shows the results of the annotation. As expected, the percentage of inadmissible phrase pairs is much higher in the first setting (random samples from phrase tables), 17.5–26.3 % compared to 7.5–9.0 %. Most phrase pairs which contributed to the final translations were valid translations (87.5–89.0 %).

The phrase table extracted from TectoMT translations was worse in both settings. However, while only 66 % of its phrase pairs were considered correct in the random selection, it was about 87 % of phrases actually used. This shows that the final decoder is able to pick the correct suggestions quite successfully.

Interestingly, despite the rather vague task description, inter-annotator agreement was quite high: 80.5 % on average in the first setting and 90.5 % in the second one.

### 3.3 Automatic Analysis of Errors in Morphology

We were interested to see whether we can find a pattern in the types of morphological errors fixed by adding the TectoMT phrase table. We translated the WMT14 test set using CH0, CH1 and CH2. We aligned each translation to the reference using HMM monolingual aligner (Zeman et al., 2011) on lemmas. We focused on cases where both the translation and the reference contain the same (aligned) lemma but the surface forms differ.[2] Table 8 shows summary statistics along with the distribution of errors among Czech parts of speech. We omitted prepositions, adverbs, conjunctions and punctuation from the table – these POSes do not really inflect in Czech.

The number of successfully matched lemmas (in the HMM alignment phase) is lowest for CH0 – this is expected as this system also got a lower BLEU score. Both other systems matched roughly 400 more lemmas within the test set (this also means 400 more opportunities for making morphological errors, i.e. CH1 and CH2 have a more difficult position than CH0 in this evaluation). The good news is that CH1 and CH2 show a significantly lower number of errors in morphology – the total number of errors was reduced by almost 500 from the 6065 made by CH0.

Overall, the number of errors per part of speech (POS) is naturally affected by the frequency of the individual POS in Czech text. We see that CH1 (and CH2) reduce the number of errors across all POSes. However, the most prominent improvement can be observed with nouns (N) and adjectives (A). We can roughly say that they account for 407 errors out of the 491 fixed by CH1.

When we look at the morphological tags for each of the 407 errors, we find that the vast majority (393 errors) *only differ in morphological case*. TectoMT therefore seems to improve target-side morphological coherence and in particular valency and noun-adjective agreement. This is further supported by the manual analysis in Section 3.4.

This analysis does not provide a good picture of the effect of adding Depfix. The difference in error numbers is negligible and inconsistent across POSes (adjectives seemingly got mildly worse while nouns were somewhat improved). Depfix rules generally prefer precision over recall, so they do not change the output considerably. Moreover, valid corrections may not be confirmed by the single reference that we have available. The accuracy of the individual Depfix rules was already evaluated by Bojar et al. (2013b). Depfix significantly improves translation quality according to human evaluation, as evidenced by Table 1.

### 3.4 Manual Analysis of TectoMT $n$-Grams

In order to check what phenomena are improved by TectoMT, we manually analyzed a small sample of $n$-grams needed by the reference and provided specifically by TectoMT, i.e. $n$-grams produced CU-TECTOMT but not CH0 and surviving to the final CH1 output. These come from the 1.5 % ✓-✓ 4-grams from Table 5.

The results are presented in Table 9. For each of the examined 4-grams, the annotator started by checking the corresponding part of CH0 output. In

[2] Due to ambiguity, the surface forms are often equal but their tags differ, we omit these cases from our analysis.

| System | # lemmas | # errors | # lemmas by part of speech | | | | |
|---|---|---|---|---|---|---|---|
| | | | A | C | N | P | V |
| CH0 | 39255 | **6065** | 1200 | 90 | 2727 | 502 | 1358 |
| CH1 | **39684** | 5574 | 1066 | 75 | 2454 | 480 | 1307 |
| CH2 | **39610** | 5559 | 1071 | 76 | 2431 | 468 | 1323 |

Table 8: Morphological errors made by Chimera divided by part of speech. A=adjective, C=numeral, N=noun, P=pronoun, V=verb.

| | |
|---|---|
| OK Anyway | 42 (31.1 %) |
| Worsened | 4 (3.0 %) |
| Bad Anyway | 2 (1.5 %) |
| Word Order esp. Syntax of Complex NPs | 13 (9.6 %) |
| Valency of Verbs and Nouns | 12 (8.9 %) |
| Agreements in NPs or Subj-Verb | 10 (7.4 %) |
| Clause Structure (Conjunctions etc.) | 8 (5.9 %) |
| Lexical Choice | 7 (5.2 %) |
| Avoided Superfluous Comma | 5 (3.7 %) |
| Possessive ('s or of) | 5 (3.7 %) |
| Properties of Verbs (number, tense, ...) | 4 (3.0 %) |
| Reflexive Particle | 3 (2.2 %) |
| Other | 20 (14.8%) |
| Total | 135 4-grams |

Table 9: Small manual analysis of 4-grams confirmed by the reference and coming from CU-TECTOMT (not produced by CH0, only by CH1).

31.1 % of cases, the CH0 output was an equally acceptable translation. (Other parts of the sentence were not considered.) The false positive 4-grams are fortunately rather rare: 3 % of these 4-grams by CH1 and confirmed by the reference are actually worse than the proposal by CH0 ("Worsened") and 1.5 % other cases are bad in both CH1 and CH0 output ("Bad Anyway").

Overall, the most frequent improvements thanks to CU-TECTOMT are related to Czech morphology, be it better choice of preposition and/or case for noun phrases dependent on verbs or other nouns ("Valency"), better preservation of case, number and/or gender within NPs or between the subject and the verb ("Agreements"), or morphological properties of verbs ("Properties of Verbs"). Another prominent class of tackled errors is related to syntax of complex noun phrases which often surface as garbled word order ("Word Order, esp. Syntax of Complex NPs"). CU-TECTOMT also helps with translating clause structure (incl. avoiding the comma used in English after topicalized elements, "Avoided Superfluous Comma"), with lexical choice, possessive constructions or the reflexive particle.

Overall, the range of improvements is rather broad, with each type receiving only a small share. The row "Other" includes diverse phenomena like better Noun-Verb-Adj disambiguation, morphological properties of nouns coming from the source, phrasal verbs, translation of numerical expressions incl. units, negation, pro-drop, or translation of named entities.

## 4 Complementary Utility

This section contains some observations on how the individual components of Chimera complement each other and to what extent one can substitute another. Unlike the previous section, we are not interested in why the components help but instead in what happens when they are not available.

### 4.1 Reachability of TectoMT Outputs for Plain Moses

In order to determine whether Moses itself could have produced the translations acquired by combining it with TectoMT, we ran a forced (constrained) decoding experiment (with table limit set to 100) – we ran CH0 on the WMT14 test set and targeted the translations produced by CH1. We first put aside the 338 sentences where the outputs of both systems are identical.

| all | different? | reachable? | score diff |
|---|---|---|---|
| 3003 | 2665 | 1741 | 1601 (<) 140 (>) |
| | | 924 | (unreachable) |
| | 338 | (identical) | |

Table 10: Forced decoding – an attempt of CH0 to reach the test set translations produced by CH1.

Out of the 2665 remaining sentences, Moses was able to produce 1741 sentences (i.e., roughly two thirds). This shows that TectoMT indeed provides many novel translations. This fact is particularly interesting when we consider the amount of data available to Moses – this year, its translation model was trained using over 52 million parallel sentences. Still, many necessary word forms are apparently missing in the phrase table (when limited to 100 options per source span).

For the reacheable sentences, we compared their model scores according to CH0. On average, the score of the CH0 original translation was slightly higher (by 1.11) than the score of the forced translation – in 1601 cases, Moses produced a better-scoring translation. We can attribute this difference to modelling errors: when we compare BLEU scores of CH1 and CH0 on these 1601 sentences, CH1 obtains a significantly better result, 24.78 vs. 23.03 (even though the model score according to CH0 is lower).

In 140 sentences, the model score of the *forced translation* was higher than the score of the translation actually produced. Apparently, the quality of CH0's output was harmed also by search errors.[3]

For completeness, we ran another variant of the forced decoding setting. We collected all phrases that were provided by the TectoMT phrase table and used by CH1 when translating the test set. We then ran constrained decoding for CH0 with these phrases as input sentences. Our question was how many of TectoMT's phrases can CH0 in principle create by itself. Out of the 15607 TectoMT's phrases used for translating the test set, CH0 was able to create 14057 of them. We looked at the roughly 10 % of phrases which were unreachable and found that some of them contained named entities or unusual formulations (not necessarily correct), however most were valid translations. Note that even if 90 % of the phrases are reachable, they can still be overly costly (esp. when built from multiple pieces) so Moses might prefer a segmentation with fewer phrases, although they match together less well.

| **table limit** | 20 | 100 | 1000 |
|---|---|---|---|
| **unreachable phrases** | 2441 | 1550 | 1210 |

Table 11: The effect of phrase table limit on the reachability of phrases in constrained decoding.

Table 11 illustrates the impact of phrase table limit on the reachability of phrases in this setting. The difference in coverage is significant between the limits 20 (the default value for Moses) and 100, which confirms our observations in Section 2.3. It is somewhat surprising that even between the 100th and 1000th best phrase translation, there are still phrases that can improve the coverage.

### 4.2 Long or Morphological LMs vs. TectoMT

In order to learn more about the interplay between the TectoMT phrase table and our language models (LMs), we carried out an experiment where we evaluated all (sensible) subsets of the LMs. For each subset, we reran tuning (MERT) and evaluated the system using BLEU.

As shown above, a significant part of the contribution of TectoMT lies in improving morphological coherence. Since the strong LMs (especially the ones trained on morphological tags) should have a similar effect, we were interested to see whether they complement each other or whether they are mutually replaceable.

In Table 12, we provide results obtained on the WMT14 test set, sorted in ascending order by the BLEU score with TectoMT included. It is immediately apparent that LMs cannot replace the contribution of TectoMT – the best result in the first column (22.69) is noticeably worse than the weakest result obtained with TectoMT included (22.93).

| **LMs** | **-TectoMT** | **+TectoMT** | Δ |
|---|---|---|---|
| long | 21.32 | 22.93 | +1.61 |
| big | 22.00 | 23.19 | +1.19 |
| long longm | 22.14 | 23.31 | +1.17 |
| long morph | 22.01 | 23.48 | +1.47 |
| long morph longm | 22.00 | 23.52 | +1.52 |
| big longm | 22.29 | 23.55 | +1.26 |
| big long | 22.26 | 23.84 | +1.58 |
| big morph | 22.21 | 23.89 | +1.68 |
| big morph longm | 22.28 | 24.01 | +1.73 |
| big long longm | **22.69** | 24.04 | +1.35 |
| big long morph | 22.48 | 24.10 | +1.62 |
| *all* | 22.59 | **24.24** | +1.65 |

Table 12: Complementary effect of adding TectoMT and language models.

Concerning the usefulness of LMs, it seems that their effects are also complementary – we get the best results by using all of them. It seems that "big" and "long" capture different aspects of the language – "big" provides very reliable statistics on short $n$-grams while "long" models common long sequences (patterns). The morphological LMs do seem correlated though. When adding "longm", our aim was to also capture long common patterns in sentential structure. However, it seems that the $n$-gram order 10 already serves this purpose quite well and extending the range provides only modest improvement.

## 5 Outstanding Issues

The current combination is quite complex and as such, it results in non-trivial interactions between the components which are hard to identify and describe. We would like to simplify the architecture somehow, striving for a clean, principled design.

[3]We also ran the same experiment with cube pruning pop limit increased to 5000. The number of sentences with lower model score decreased to 28.

However, as we have shown, we cannot simply remove any of the components without a significant loss of translation quality, so this remains an open question for further research.

### 5.1 Weaknesses of CHO

On many occassions, we were surprised by the low quality of CHO's translations. We considered this system a rather strong baseline, given the LMs trained on billions of tokens and the factored scheme, which specifically targets morphological coherence. Yet we observed many obvious errors both in lexical choice and morphological agreement, which were well within the scope of the phrase length limit and $n$-gram order. We believe that more sophisticated statistical models, such as discriminative classifiers which take source context into account (Carpuat and Wu, 2007) or operation sequence models (Durrani et al., 2011), could be applied to further improve CHO.

### 5.2 Practical Considerations

As he have shown, our approach to system combination has some unique properties and can certainly be an interesting alternative. Yet it can be viewed as impractical – the models (the TectoMT phrase table, specifically) actually require the input to be known in advance. In this section, we outline a possible solution which would allow for using the system in an on-line setting.

The synthetic parallel data consist of the dev set and test set. Our development data can be fixed in advance so re-tuning the system parameters is not required for new inputs.

The only remaining issue is ensuring that the second phrase table contains the TectoMT translation of the input. We propose to first translate the input sentence using TectoMT. Then for word alignment, we can either use the alignment information directly from TectoMT or apply a pre-trained word-alignment model, provided e.g. by MGiza (Gao and Vogel, 2008). Phrase extraction and scoring can be done quickly on the fly.

Phrase scores should ideally be combined with the dev-set part of the phrase table. Moses has support for dynamic updating of its phrase tables (Bertoldi, 2014), so changing the scores or adding new phrase pairs is possible at very little cost.

With pre-trained word alignment and dynamic updating of the phrase table, we believe that our approach could be readily deployed in practice.

## 6 Conclusion

We have carefully analyzed the system combination Chimera which consists of a statistical system Moses (CHO), a deep-syntactic transfer-based system TectoMT and a rule-based post-processing tool Depfix. We focused on the interaction between CHO and CU-TECTOMT. We described several techniques for inspecting this combination, based on both automatic and manual evaluation.

We have found that the transfer-based component provides a mix of useful, correct translations and noise. Many of its translations are unavailable to the statistical component, so its generalization power is in fact essential. Moses is able to select the useful translations quite successfully thanks to strong language models, which are trained both on surface forms and morphological tags.

Our experiment with forced decoding further showed that translations which are reachable for Moses are often not chosen due to modelling errors. It is the extra prominence these translations get thanks to CU-TECTOMT that helps to overcome these errors.

We show that our approach to system combination (using translations from the transfer-based system as additional training data) has several advantageous properties and that it might be an interesting alternative to standard techniques. We outline a solution to the issue of the practical applicability of our method.

Overall, we find that by adding the transfer-based system, we obtain novel translations and improved morphological coherence. The final translation quality is improved significantly over both CHO and CU-TECTOMT alone, setting the state of the art for English→Czech translation for several years in a row.


## Acknowledgements

This research was supported by the grants H2020-ICT-2014-1-645452 (QT21), H2020-ICT-2014-1-644402 (HimL), H2020-ICT-2014-1-644753 (KConnect), SVV 260 224 and GAUK 1356213. This work has been using language resources developed, stored and distributed by the LINDAT/CLARIN project of the Ministry of Education, Youth and Sports of the Czech Republic (project LM2010013).

## References


Loic Barrault. 2010. MANY, Open Source Machine Translation System Combination. In *Prague Bulletin of Mathematical Linguistics - Special Issue on Open Source Machine Translation Tools*, number 93 in Prague Bulletin of Mathematical Linguistics. Charles University, January.

Nicola Bertoldi. 2014. Dynamic models in moses for online adaptation. *The Prague Bulletin of Mathematical Linguistics*, 101(1):7–28.

Ondřej Bojar and Aleš Tamchyna. 2011. Improving Translation Model by Monolingual Data. In *Proc. of WMT*, pages 330–336. ACL.

Ondřej Bojar, Kamil Kos, and David Mareček. 2010. Tackling Sparse Data Issue in Machine Translation Evaluation. In *Proceedings of the ACL 2010 Conference Short Papers*, pages 86–91, Uppsala, Sweden, July. Association for Computational Linguistics.

Ondřej Bojar, Christian Buck, Chris Callison-Burch, Christian Federmann, Barry Haddow, Philipp Koehn, Christof Monz, Matt Post, Radu Soricut, and Lucia Specia. 2013a. Findings of the 2013 Workshop on Statistical Machine Translation. In *Eighth Workshop on Statistical Machine Translation*, WMT, pages 1–44, Sofia, Bulgaria.

Ondřej Bojar, Rudolf Rosa, and Aleš Tamchyna. 2013b. Chimera – Three Heads for English-to-Czech Translation. In *Proceedings of the Eighth Workshop on Statistical Machine Translation*, pages 90–96.

Ondřej Bojar, Christian Buck, Christian Federmann, Barry Haddow, Philipp Koehn, Johannes Leveling, Christof Monz, Pavel Pecina, Matt Post, Herve Saint-Amand, et al. 2014. Findings of the 2014 workshop on statistical machine translation. In *Proceedings of the Ninth Workshop on Statistical Machine Translation*, pages 12–58. Association for Computational Linguistics Baltimore, MD, USA.

Marine Carpuat and Dekai Wu. 2007. Improving statistical machine translation using word sense disambiguation. In *Proceedings of the 2007 Joint Conference on Empirical Methods in Natural Language Processing and Computational Natural Language Learning (EMNLP-CoNLL)*, Prague, Czech Republic.

Jonathan H. Clark, Chris Dyer, Alon Lavie, and Noah A. Smith. 2011. Better hypothesis testing for statistical machine translation: Controlling for optimizer instability. In *Proc. of ACL/HLT*, pages 176–181. ACL.

Marta R. Costa-jussà and José A.R. Fonollosa. 2015. Latest trends in hybrid machine translation and its applications. *Computer Speech and Language*, 32(1):3–10. Hybrid Machine Translation: integration of linguistics and statistics.

Nadir Durrani, Helmut Schmid, and Alexander M. Fraser. 2011. A joint sequence translation model with integrated reordering. In Dekang Lin, Yuji Matsumoto, and Rada Mihalcea, editors, *ACL*, pages 1045–1054. The Association for Computer Linguistics.

Qin Gao and Stephan Vogel. 2008. Parallel Implementations of Word Alignment Tool. In *Software Engineering, Testing, and Quality Assurance for Natural Language Processing*, SETQA-NLP '08, pages 49–57. ACL.

Kenneth Heafield and Alon Lavie. 2010. Combining Machine Translation Output with Open Source, The Carnegie Mellon Multi-Engine Machine Translation Scheme. In *Prague Bulletin of Mathematical Linguistics - Special Issue on Open Source Machine Translation Tools*, number 93 in Prague Bulletin of Mathematical Linguistics. Charles University, January.

Philipp Koehn, Hieu Hoang, Alexandra Birch, Chris Callison-Burch, Marcello Federico, Nicola Bertoldi, Brooke Cowan, Wade Shen, Christine Moran, Richard Zens, et al. 2007. Moses: Open source toolkit for statistical machine translation. In *Proceedings of the 45th annual meeting of the ACL on interactive poster and demonstration sessions*, pages 177–180. Association for Computational Linguistics.

Evgeny Matusov, Gregor Leusch, Rafael E. Banchs, Nicola Bertoldi, Daniel Dechelotte, Marcello Federico, Muntsin Kolss, Young-Suk Lee, Jose B. Marino, Matthias Paulik, Salim Roukos, Holger Schwenk, and Hermann Ney. 2008. System Combination for Machine Translation of Spoken and Written Language. *IEEE Transactions on Audio, Speech and Language Processing*, 16(7):1222–1237, September.

Franz Josef Och. 2003. Minimum Error Rate Training in Statistical Machine Translation. In *Proc. of the Association for Computational Linguistics*, Sapporo, Japan, July 6-7.

Martin Popel and Zdeněk Žabokrtský. 2010. TectoMT: Modular NLP Framework. In Hrafn Loftsson, Eirikur Rögnvaldsson, and Sigrun Helgadottir, editors, *IceTAL 2010*, volume 6233 of *LNCS*, pages 293–304. Iceland Centre for Language Technology (ICLT), Springer.

Rudolf Rosa, David Mareček, and Ondřej Dušek. 2012. DEPFIX: A system for automatic correction of Czech MT outputs. In *Proc. of WMT*, pages 362–368. ACL.

Aleš Tamchyna, Martin Popel, Rudolf Rosa, and Ondřej Bojar. 2014. CUNI in WMT14: Chimera still awaits bellerophon. In *Proceedings of the Ninth Workshop on Statistical Machine Translation*, pages 195–200, Baltimore, MD, USA. Association for Computational Linguistics.

Daniel Zeman, Mark Fishel, Jan Berka, and Ondřej Bojar. 2011. Addicter: What is wrong with my translations? *The Prague Bulletin of Mathematical Linguistics*, 96:79–88.

# Establishing sentential structure via realignments from small parallel corpora

**George Tambouratzis**
ILSP/Athena Res. Centre
6 Artemidos & Epidavrou,
Paradissos Amaroussiou,
Athens, GR-15125, Greece.
giorg_t@ilsp.gr

**Vasiliki Pouli**
ILSP/Athena Res. Centre
6 Artemidos & Epidavrou,
Paradissos Amaroussiou,
Athens, GR-15125, Greece.
vpouli@ilsp.gr

**Abstract**

The present article reports on efforts to improve the translation accuracy of a corpus–based hybrid MT system developed using the PRESEMT methodology. This methodology operates on a phrasal basis, where phrases are linguistically-motivated but are automatically determined via a dedicated module. Here, emphasis is placed on improving the structure of each translated sentence, by replacing the Example-Based MT approach originally used in PRESEMT with a sub-sentential approach. Results indicate that an improved accuracy can be achieved, as measured by objective metrics.

## 1 Introduction

In the present article, a corpus-based methodology is studied, which allows the creation of MT systems for a variety of languages using a common set of software modules. This methodology has been specifically designed to address the scarcity of parallel corpora needed to train for instance a Statistical Machine Translation system (Koehn, 2010), in particular for less widely-resourced languages. Thus the main source of information is a large collection of monolingual corpora in the target language (TL). This collection is supplemented by a small parallel corpus of no more than a few hundred sentences, which the methodology employs to extract information about the structural transfer from the source language (SL) to the target one. The aim in the present article is to investigate how the translation quality can be improved over the best results reported so far (Tambouratzis et al., 2014). Emphasis is placed on extracting the salient information from the small parallel corpus, to most accurately define the structure of the sentences being translated. The efficacy of this effort is verified by a set of experiments.

## 2 Summary of Translation Process

The PRESEMT methodology studied here is designed to address the very limited availability of parallel corpora (of a few hundred sentences at most) with large amounts of monolingual corpora, and achieve a competitive translation quality without explicit provision of linguistic knowledge. Instead, linguistic knowledge is extracted from the corpora available, via algorithmic means (Sofianopoulos et al., 2012). The parallel corpus comprises a number of aligned sentences (these are referred to as ACS Aligned Corpus Sentences).

The PRESEMT methodology comprises two phases, which process the text to be translated on a sentence-by-sentence basis. The first phase determines the structure of the translation (Phase 1–Structure selection phase) using the parallel corpus. The second phase rearranges the sequence of tokens in each phrase and decides on the optimal translation of each token (Phase 2 – Translation equivalent selection).

PRESEMT adopts a phrase-based approach, where the phrases are syntactically motivated and the text-to-be-translated is processed on the basis of the phrases contained. These phrases are determined in a pre-processing phase, just before the beginning of the translation process, via the Phrase Model Generator (PMG) module. PMG is trained on the small parallel corpus to port the phrasing scheme from the target language (in which a chunker is available) towards the source language. Thus PMG is able to chunk arbitrary



*Proceedings of the ACL 2015 Fourth Workshop on Hybrid Approaches to Translation (HyTra)*, pages 21–29,
Beijing, China, July 31, 2015. ©2015 Association for Computational Linguistics

input sentences into phrases, in the process eliminating the need for a suitable SL chunker.

As a result, in the first translation phase each input sentence (*InS*) is handled as a sequence of phrases. The reordering of these phrases in the TL translation is determined by comparing the *InS* structure to the SL-side structures of all sentences of the parallel corpus. To this end, a Dynamic Time Warping (DTW) algorithm, as discussed in Myers et al. (1980), is used. The DTW implementation chosen is that of Smith et al. (1981), with all comparisons being performed on a phrase-by-phrase basis, on the SL-side. When the best-matching SL-side sentence structure is determined, the structure of the *InS* translation is defined by the corresponding TL-side sentence. This process is summarized in Fig.1.

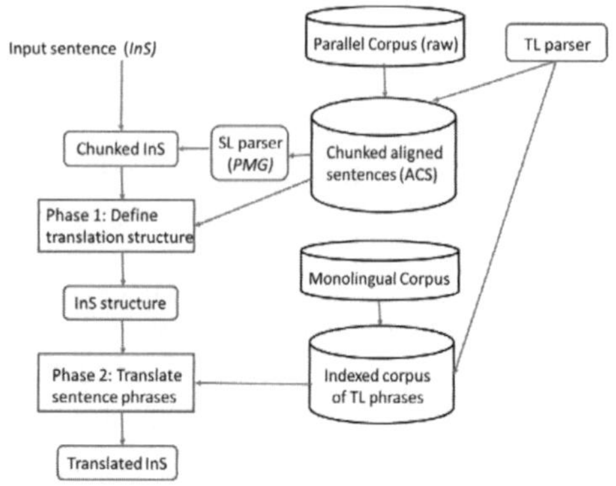


Figure 1: Schematic description of PRESEMT translation methodology.

In turn, Phase 2 samples the indexed monolingual TL corpus to determine the most likely token translations and sequence of tokens within the boundaries of each phrase, using the stable-marriage algorithm (Mairson, 1992). The PRESEMT translation methodology is of a hybrid nature, as Phase 1 is EBMT-inspired (Nagao, 1984 & Hutchins, 2005), while Phase 2 is conceptually much closer to SMT (Brown et al., 1988).

In the present article, emphasis is placed on improving specifically the first translation phase, aiming for an improvement in the resulting quality. The aim is to algorithmically establish realignment rules that cover sub-sentential segments. Conceptually, this possesses similarities to the preordering methods proposed for SMT systems (cf. Lerner et al., 2013 and Stymne, 2009). In (Lerner et al., 2013) preordering is aimed to pre-process the input text so as to render the sequence in SL closer to the sequence in TL. This can simplify the translation process significantly, and result in improved translation scores. However, a dependency parser in the SL-side is assumed and preordering is performed prior to any processing of the input string to simplify the training of the SMT.

On the contrary, in the present article the aim is to determine sub-sentential re-orderings which are applied within the translation process. Furthermore, in PRESEMT the SL-side parsing scheme is induced via the TL-side shallow parser and thus is not sufficiently detailed to provide subject-object relationships or to determine dependencies as required by preordering algorithms. Finally, as the parallel corpus only numbers a few hundred sentences, the SL-side information is not sufficiently extensive to support the extraction of large numbers of rules as reported by e.g. Stymne (2009).

## 3 Porting the Sentence Structure from SL to TL

The structure selection phase serves to determine for each sentence to be translated the structure of the translation. For each phrase in the sentence, the following tuple is created:

$$phr_i = [phr\_type_i; pos(head_i); case(head_i)] \quad (1)$$

where $phr\_type_i$ indicates the phrase-type of the $i^{th}$ phrase, $pos(head_i)$ is the Part-of-Speech (PoS) tag of the phrase head, and $case(head_i)$ is the case of the phrase head. Then the $k^{th}$ sentence is expressed as an ordered sequence of $j$ tuples:

$$struct(sent_k) = [phr_1; phr_2; ..; phr_j] \quad (2)$$

To determine the optimal structure of the translated sentence *InS*, the information existing in the small parallel corpus of $N$ sentences is exploited. More specifically, this corpus contains a number of $N$ aligned sentences ACS (Aligned Corpus Sentences), for which the SL and the TL sentence are direct equivalents of each other (denoted as *ACS_SL* and *ACS_TL* respectively). Then, the structure of the *InS* translation is the one of the $c^{th}$ sentence pair ACS, for which the following expression is maximized:

$$\max_{1 \le i \le N} \{simil(struct(InS), struct(ACS\_SL_i)\} \quad (3)$$

In (3), *simil* expresses the phrase-wise structural similarity between sentences *InS* and *ACS_SL* determined via a phrase-by-phrase comparison (as discussed in Sofianopoulos at el., 2012). The similarity of two phrases is calculated as the weighted sum of three constituent similarities, (a) the phrase type, (b) the phrase head PoS tag and (c) the grammatical case of the phrase head.

### 3.1 Analysing translation problems

An analysis of PRESEMT results has shown that a large proportion of translation errors are due to the first phase of the translation process. In such cases, the structure of the translation of an input sentence *InS* fails to be accurately determined, and the translation quality suffers accordingly. It should be noted that within the PRESEMT system, the diversity of sentences in the parallel corpus is limited. Due to the limited size of the parallel corpus, the number of archetypes supporting the transfer of structures from SL to TL is smaller than is desirable.

To indicate the effect of the limited coverage provided by the restricted number of parallel SL-TL sentence pairs, an example is provided in Figure 2, based on the Greek-to-English translation pair. In this example only the phrase types are quoted, without any additional differentiation (such as case or PoS of the phrase head). In this example, the original sentence in Greek is shown in (1) while in (2) and (3) the translation is shown in terms of lemmas and tokens, when using the standard Structure selection algorithm of PRESEMT. In (4) and (5), the translation using our proposed novel structure selection algorithm is shown, which has an improved structure.

<table>
<tr><th colspan="2">(1) Initial Sentence</th></tr>
<tr><td colspan="2">PC2(Ο πατέρας της) VC6(προσπαθεί) ADVC8(μάταια) να PC11(τη) VC13(μεταπείσει) .</td></tr>
<tr><th colspan="2">Standard Structure Selection</th></tr>
<tr><th>(2) Lemmas</th><th>(3) Tokens</th></tr>
<tr><td>PC2(her father) VC6(try) ADVC8(in vain) to PC11(her) VC13(dissuade).</td><td>Her father tries in vain to her dissuade.</td></tr>
<tr><th colspan="2">Proposed Structure Selection</th></tr>
<tr><th>(4) Lemmas</th><th>(5) Tokens</th></tr>
<tr><td>PC2(her father) VC6(try) ADVC8(in vain) to VC13(dissuade) PC11(her).</td><td>Her father tries in vain to dissuade her.</td></tr>
</table>

Figure 2: translation of input sentence (1) as generated by the standard PRESEMT structure selection [cf.(2) and (3)] & the new one [cf.(4) and (5)] in terms of lemmas and tokens respectively.

For this language pair, four phrase types exist (namely ADVC, PC, VC and ADJC), as determined by the Treetagger (Schmid, 1995) version for the English language. To simplify the analysis, it is assumed that all sentences have a fixed structure size k (that is, they comprise exactly k phrases each). Then, the number of possible combinations, $N_{phr}$ depends on the number of phrase types *ptype* (not taking into account linguistic constraints that may render certain combinations ungrammatical):

$$N_{phr} = ptype^{k} \qquad (4)$$

In the case of only four phrase types and a sequence of ten phrases, the number of combinations as determined by eqn. (1) is $4^{10}$, which is approximately equal to $10^6$. However, the size of the parallel corpus in PRESEMT is typically constrained to only 200 sentences. Consequently, for the EBMT approach used by PRESEMT, the maximum number of possible structural transformations from SL to TL is at most 200. In reality there are bound to be identical entries within the structures of the aligned sentences, ACS, with more than one sentence pairs having the same structure in terms of phrase sequences in both SL and TL. For instance, in the default parallel corpus of 200 sentences used in the Greek-to-English PRESEMT system, the actual number of unique SL/TL phrase-based structures (defined as a sequence of phrase types) is approximately 100. Hence, the population of archetypes covers the pattern space much more sparsely than is ideal, and the likelihood of a representative exemplar existing in the small parallel corpus is very low.

On the basis of this observation, it is expected that for several input sentences *InS* a sub-optimal match will be established, as either no satisfactory match can be found or only a partial match will be determined, with conflicts occurring for one or more phrases. For instance, for a given 4-phrase input sentence with structure {PC ; VC ; ADVC; PC} the closest match may well be archetype {PC ; VC ; PC ; PC}, resulting in a mismatch at the third element. As a result the structure of the translation is defined by making arbitrary approximations, due to the constrained corpus size. If the proportion of mismatches is very high, it might be preferable to disregard the structural transformations indicated by the chosen template as they are probably inaccurate.

### 3.2 Replacing the classic structure selection

Based on the aforementioned discussion, the question becomes how to use more effectively the information inherent in the small parallel corpus of SL-TL sentences, to determine realignments when translating sentences from SL to TL. In the original Structure selection algorithm an EBMT-type algorithm (Nagao, 1984) is used where a single sentence from the parallel corpus defines the structure of the translation, implicitly assuming an appropriate coverage of the pattern space. An alternative approach is investigated in the present article, where from each sentence pair of the parallel corpus, knowledge is extracted about realignments of phrases when transferring a sentence from SL to TL. Thus sub-sentential templates (hereafter termed **realignment templates**) are created which describe the necessary reorderings of phrases for relatively short sequences in preference to longer templates that operate on the entire sentence (as is the case in the standard Structure selection). The aim then becomes to extract a representative set of such templates that is applicable to the large majority of sentences.

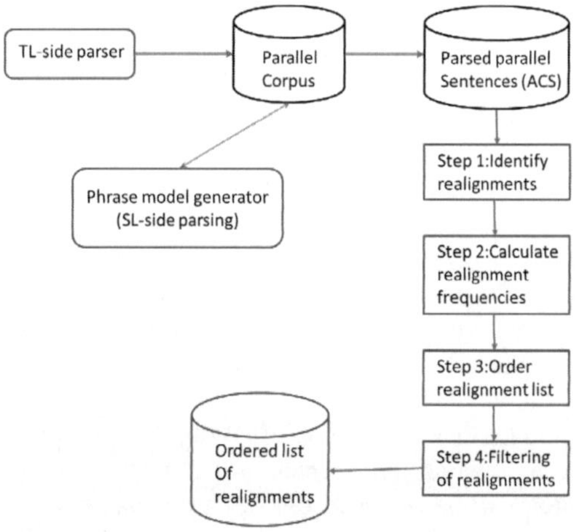


Figure 3: Sequence of steps to extract realignment templates from a parallel corpus.

The underlying assumption of this approach is that when translating from SL to TL, the structure should not be modified, in the absence of evidence that a realignment is required. Hence, the aim is to determine templates that model phrase realignments between the SL and TL sides, and which are then applied to the input sentence structure depending on certain criteria. An example of such phenomena includes the subject which in Greek may follow the corresponding verb chunk, though in English this order is reversed. What is needed is to determine realignments that consistently occur when transitioning from SL to TL and to estimate their corresponding likelihood. Regarding the linguistic resources available, this information may only be extracted from the small parallel corpus. The criteria for estimating the likelihood comprise:

- the length of the realignment template in terms of phrases,
- the frequency of occurrence of the template in the small parallel corpus.

A different realignment template is defined for each reordering of phrase sequences, from the SL and TL side sentences. To support direct comparisons with earlier results, each phrase is defined by the phrase type (e.g. verb phrase or noun phrase), the phrase head part-of-speech (PoS) tag and its case (if this exists for the given language). Of course, additional characteristics may also be chosen, depending on the specific language pairs studied, to attain a better performance.

The outline of the algorithm to create a set of realignment templates is depicted in Figure 3. Initially (in Step 1) every parallel sentence pair is scanned to find phrase realignments, and each realignment is recorded in a list. Then (in Step 2), identical realignments (where sequences of phrases in both SL and TL match exactly) are assimilated to record the frequency of occurrence of each realignment template. In Step 3, a heuristic is used to score each one of the templates and a new ordered list of templates is created. Based on the heuristic, a higher score indicates a higher likelihood of correct activation. Finally, a filtering Step 4 is used to eliminate templates that are considered unlikely to be correct, based on their frequency of occurrence in the parallel corpus (more details on the heuristic function and filtering process are provided in sub-section 3.4). The resulting list of templates is then used to define the structure of the input sentence *InS* when translated, by consecutively trying to apply each of the realignment templates, one at a time, starting with the highest-ranked one, as discussed in the next sub-section.

### 3.3 Application of realignment templates

When ordering the realignment templates, two distinct cases are defined, depending on whether context beyond the realignment template is taken into account. In the first case, the algorithm identifies the realignment template by finding only the sequence of phrases that are realigned, without taking into account the identities of any neighbouring phrases (this being denoted as "Align-nC", where nC stands for No Context).

In the second case, the context of the realignment template to the left and the right is also considered. Thus, one additional phrase to the left and to the right is recorded within an extended realignment template. In this approach, three distinct variants are considered, depending on the degree of the context match. More specifically:

a. If the left and right contexts need to fully-match (i.e. the type of phrases need to coincide but the PoS tag and case of the phrase heads also need to agree), this is termed as **type-0** (and is denoted as "Align-C0", where C0 stands for Context-type-0). This type of match is the most restrictive as it requires matching of all characteristics but on the other hand it allows for more finely-detailed matching.

b. If the left and right context need to be matched only in terms of the type of phrases (but not the PoS tag and case of the phrase heads), this is termed as **type-1** (denoted as "Align-C1"). In contrast to context phrases, for the phrases within the realignment templates, matching extends to both the PoS tag and case of the phrase head. The alignment of type-1 is thus relaxed in comparison to that of type-0 in terms of context-defining phrases, allowing a potentially larger number of matches of the alignment template to the parallel corpus, as observed in Table 1.

c. If for both the context and realignment phrases, only the phrase type is required to match, (i.e. not the head PoS tag or its case) then this is termed as **type-2**, (denoted as "Align-C2") and corresponds to the least restrictive match in terms of the context, giving the largest number of matches, as seen in Table 1. However, this relaxation in matching might allow for realignment cases where the PoS tags of the phrases and their neighboring ones do not match, thus resulting in lower translation accuracy.

Table 1: increase of realignments detected for different variations with context in comparison to the no-context (Align-nC) case, for the standard Greek-to-English parallel corpus.

| Realignment variations | | | |
|---|---|---|---|
| **Align-nC** | **Align-C0** | **Align-C1** | **Align-C2** |
| +0% | +75% | +150% | +825% |

Two examples of realignment templates extracted from a small parallel corpus are depicted in Figure 4. For a specific realignment, the different realignment templates extracted with and without context are depicted in Figure 5.

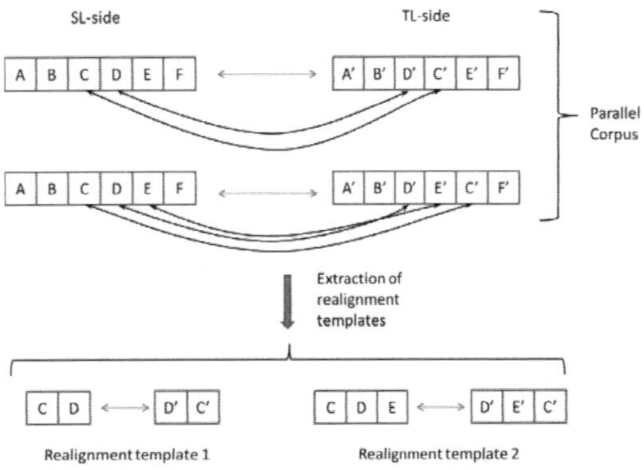


Figure 4: Examples of realignment templates.

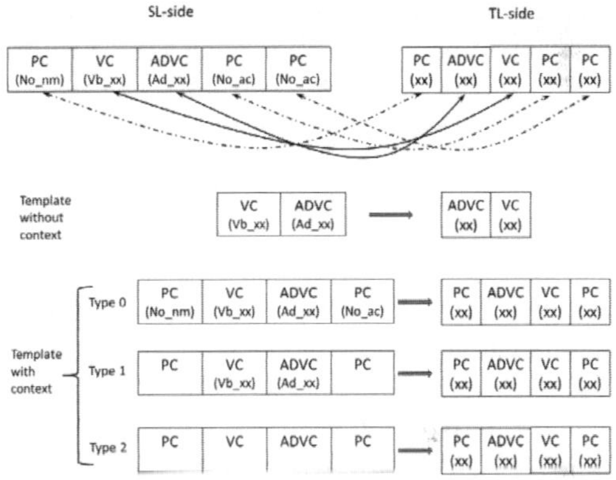


Figure 5: Types of realignment template without context and with context – the parallel SL/TL sentence is shown on top, followed by the different templates that can be extracted.

The optimal matching depends of course on the characteristics of the language pair being handled, as well as the amount of training data available. Thus more discriminative templates can be established, provided that the appropriate amount of training data is available. Else, it is likely that most templates will only be encountered once, and effectively a look-up table will be established for realignment templates found within the parallel corpus. In this case, no generalization by the system will be possible and the translation accuracy can be expected to suffer. Comparative performances of the aforementioned variants will be discussed in the experimental results' section.

### 3.4 Heuristic function for ranking realignment templates

The heuristic function has a key role in determining the system behavior, by defining the appropriate ranking of the templates. As the system attempts to iteratively match the sequence of phrases in the chunked input sentences with each realignment template, it first applies the highest-ranked templates and progressively moves to lower-ranked ones. A lower-ranked template is applied to a specific set of phrases provided that no higher-ranked template has been applied to any of these phrases. Thus, the ranking dictates the selection of one realignment template over another, and can affect the accuracy of the translation structure.

Based on a preliminary study, it was decided to rank higher realignment templates which occur more frequently within the given training set (parallel corpus). Also, the application of larger templates is preferred over smaller ones. The actual heuristic function chosen for translation simulations is expressed by equation (5):

$$score_i = freq_i + a_1 * len_i \quad (5)$$

Where $score_i$ is the score of the *i-th* realignment template, $freq_i$ corresponds to the frequency of occurrence of the template in the training corpus and $len_i$ is the length of the realignment template in terms of phrases. Parameter $a_1$ is used to weigh the two factors appropriately.

In addition, a number of constraints serve to eliminate cases where potentially spurious realignments may be chosen as valid ones. These constraints have been developed by studying initial translation results. For this description, a realignment between the SL and TL-sides is defined as $rseq_{SL-TL}$. On the other hand, $rseq_{SL}$ is used to denote only the part of the realignment in the SL-side of the parallel corpus.

Constraint 1: If a realignment involving a sequence of phrases $rseq_{SL-TL}$ is encountered very infrequently in comparison to the occurrences of the sequence in the SL-side of the parallel corpus, $rseq_{SL}$, then it is rejected. The aim of this constraint is to eliminate unlikely realignments, which are not applicable for the majority of SL-side patterns [1]. This is expressed by (6), where $freq\_thres$ is a user-defined threshold:

$$\frac{freq(rseq_{SL-TL})}{freq(rseq_{SL})} \geq freq\_thres \quad (6)$$

Constraint 2: If a realignment $rseq_{SL-TL}$ occurs in the parallel corpus only very rarely, then it is removed from the list of applicable realignments. This is implemented by setting a minimum threshold value *min_freq* for a realignment template to be retained, allowing the reorderings that are rarely applied to specific phrase sequences to be filtered out.

Constraint 3 (hapax legomena): This constraint refines the elimination process of realignments dictated by Constraint 2. More specifically, it introduces an exception to Constraint 2, to prevent certain realignment templates from being filtered-out. If the filtering-out concerns a sequence $rseq_{SL-TL}$ that appears only once in the parallel corpus SL-side, Constraint 3 is activated to retain this rare realignment.

## 4 Experiments

### 4.1 Experimental Setup

In the present article, the Greek-to-English language pair is used for experimentation. To ensure compatibility with earlier results, the standard language resources of PRESEMT are used, including the basic parallel corpus of 200 sentences and the two test sets of 200 sentences each, denoted as testsetA and testsetB (all these resources have been retrieved from the www.presemt.eu website). Regarding the parameters related to the realignment templates, the value used for *freq_thres* is 0.50, while *min_freq* is set to 3. Finally, parameter $a_1$ of eqn (5) is set to 100 for the given experiments, indicating a strong preference to larger realignment templates. These parameter values have been chosen by performing trial simulations during the development phase.

Different PMG modules resulting in different phrase sizes have been studied to investigate alternative SL phrasing schemes applied on the sentences to be translated. This test is performed, to determine whether the proposed realignment method is robust. Comparative evaluation with a selection of PMG modules with different phrase sizes can indicate the effectiveness of realignment templates in this MT methodology. Experiments are performed by considering or not the context (cases: Align-nC, Align-C) or by varying

[1] In contrast to training, where both SL and TL information is available, during operation only the SL-side pattern is available and the TL-side one is unknown. Thus an infrequent realignment cannot be relied upon to provide structure-defining information.

the type of match when Align-C is applied (cases: Align-C0, Align-C1, Align-C2). The best realignments have been compared to the baseline i.e. the case when the classic Structure selection algorithm is used (Tambouratzis et al., 2014).

Regarding the PMG modules, the first version, termed PMG-s gives the highest reported translation accuracy (Tambouratzis, 2014), splitting sentences into smaller phrases[2]. The alternative PMG (PMG-b) evaluated, favours larger phrases than PMG-s and results in smaller average sentence lengths expressed in terms of phrases. The average sentence sizes for each phrasing scheme in both testsets can be seen in Table 2, while the numbers of realignment templates applied to the input sets for testsets A and B are detailed in Table 3. The difference in realignments between the two testsets reflects the fact that TestsetA has smaller sentences of on average 15.3 words per sentence, while for TestsetB this is 22.6 words (the sentence size being increased by 48% in terms of words). Hence, the occurrence of realignments is higher for TestsetB.

Table 2: Average sentence sizes in terms of phrases for the two evaluation testsets when different PMG modules are applied.

| | PMG-s | PMG-b |
|---|---|---|
| TestsetA | 6.90 | 6.21 |
| TestsetB | 10.64 | 9.66 |

Table 3: Total number of realignments recorded per testset, for different realignment variations.

| TestsetA | Realignment variations | | | |
|---|---|---|---|---|
| | Align-nC | Align-C0 | Align-C1 | Align-C2 |
| PMG-s | 4 | 7 | 10 | 37 |
| PMG-b | 11 | 11 | 14 | 38 |

| TestsetB | Realignment variations | | | |
|---|---|---|---|---|
| | Align-nC | Align-C0 | Align-C1 | Align-C2 |
| PMG-s | 7 | 9 | 18 | 76 |
| PMG-b | 7 | 10 | 16 | 59 |

MT setups are evaluated regarding the translation quality, based on a selection of widely-used MT metrics: BLEU (Papineni et al., 2002), NIST (NIST, 2002), Meteor (Denkowski et al., 2011) and TER (Snover et al., 2006). For BLEU, NIST and Meteor, the score measures the translation accuracy and a higher score indicates a better translation. For TER the score counts the error rate and thus a lower score indicates a more successful translation. For reasons of uniformity, when comparing scores, an improvement in a metric is depicted as a positive change (for all metrics, including TER).

### 4.2 Experimental Results

Fig. 6 depicts the BLEU scores for different phrasing schemes when the different cases and variations of the realignments are applied (cases: Align-nC, Align-C0, Align-C1, Align-C2). As observed, the PMG-s variant achieves the highest score in general and especially when neighboring phrases are not taken into account (Align-nC BLEU score = 0.3626), thus not limiting the realignments to specific environments.

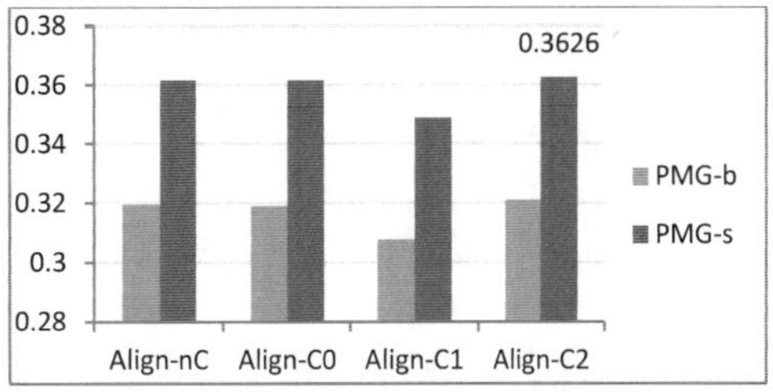


Figure 6: BLEU scores for the different realignment cases, for both PMGs and Testset A.

Figure 7 indicates how translation quality is improved when the best realignment case (Align-nC) is applied compared to the baseline, for different PMGs, using TestsetA. The use of realignments improves metric scores in both PMGs, indicating the improved robustness of the MT system towards this choice. The highest improvement of 1.63% observed for the BLEU score is obtained with PMG-s, which leads to sentences of larger length (with more phrases but of fewer words each).

When applying the best realignment variant (Align-nC) to TestsetB with the two phrasing schemes (i.e. PMG-s, PMG-b) a substantial improvement is achieved, reaching 1.12% for BLEU (cf. Figure 8). As before, PMG-s achieves the greatest improvement, showing that the realignment template algorithm benefits to a greater degree phrasing schemes that generate larger numbers of phrases per sentence.

[2] Based on the experiments reported in (Tambouratzis, 2014) both PMG-s and PMG-b correspond to criterion $C_F$, the differentiation being that PMG-b (PMG-s) allows (prevents) the formation of phrases containing multiple cases.

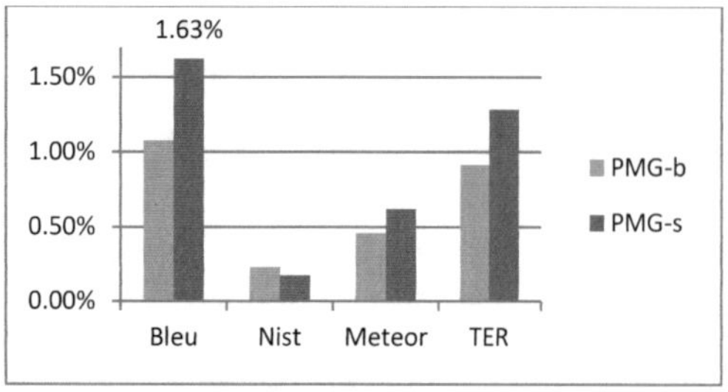


Figure 7: Improvement in scores for the Align-nC case compared to the baseline, for the two phrasing schemes when applied to TestsetA.

A further evaluation effort has involved examining how the proposed realignment template method compares to a zero-baseline, where the SL structure is retained without change in TL. In this case, the improvement amounts to 0.53% in terms of the BLEU score.

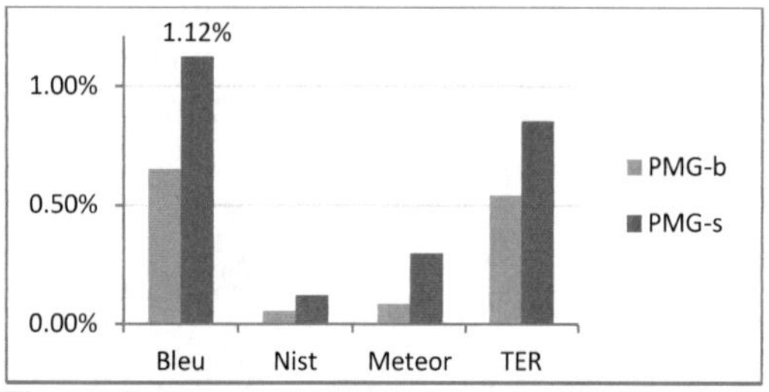


Figure 8: Improvement in scores for Align-nC case compared to the baseline, when the two phrasing schemes are applied to TestsetB.

To compare against another benchmark, TestSetA was translated with a MOSES-based SMT (trained with a parallel corpus of approx. 1.2 million sentences - the parallel corpus is 4 orders of magnitude larger than that used by PRESEMT) and resulted in BLEU and NIST scores of 0.3795 and 7.039 respectively. These MOSES scores are comparable to the scores achieved by PRESEMT with Align-nC (0.3626 and 7.086 for BLEU and NIST respectively).

### 4.3 Statistical Analysis of Results

To determine whether the results are statistically significant, paired-sample T-tests were applied at a sentence level. Comparing the use of realignment templates with and without context (Align-nC versus Align-C2), the scores for each of the 200 sentences were used to form two distinct populations for TestsetA. By comparing the two populations, for both PMG-b and PMG-s, a statistically significant difference is found at a confidence level of 95%, showing that Align-nC gives a significantly better translation quality over Align-C2. On the other hand, the improvement of Align-nC compared to the baseline scenario is small, thus not resulting in statistically significant differences.

## 5 Conclusions and Future Work

The proposed method of applying realignments to sentence structure has been shown to provide a useful increase in translation accuracy over the best configurations established in earlier experiments. Still, a number of possible extensions of the work presented here have been identified. These focus primarily on how to extract a more comprehensive set of templates from the limited-size parallel corpus available. To achieve this, one method would be to integrate linguistic knowledge. For instance, by identifying grammatical categories (i.e. different PoS tags) which are equivalent, it is possible to extend knowledge to introduce new realignment templates based on known ones and thus cover more cases.

Also, it is possible to concatenate different realignment templates to larger groups, in order to make more accurate calculations of the statistics underlying each template. For instance, it may be assumed that whether the PoS tag of the phrase head is a noun or pronoun, the template remains the same and such cases can be grouped together. By extrapolating these new templates, an increase in the pattern space coverage can be expected, leading to an improved translation accuracy.

A point which is of interest is applicability to other language pairs. As is the case for the PRESEMT MT methodology as a whole, a key decision was not to design the methodology for one specific language pair. For instance, initial experimentation has shown that the application of realignment templates has correctly generated templates for the case of split verbs when German is the TL (here the Greek-to-German language pair). This is important, as split verbs have been identified as one of the key problems when translating into German. Of course, more experimentation is needed in terms of the generalisation abilities of such realignment templates to cover more cases than those encountered in the training set, and to efficiently model the shift of the second part of the verb to the end of the relevant sentence. Still, the ability of the proposed realignment template method to identify such occurrences is promising.

## Acknowledgements

The research reported in this article has been funded partly by a number of projects including the PRESEMT project (ICT-FP7-Call4/248307) and the POLYTROPON project (KRIPIS-GSRT, MIS: 448306).

The authors wish to acknowledge the assistance of Ms. M. Vassiliou of ILSP/Athena R.C. on the setting up of experiments and of Dr. S. Sofianopoulos of ILSP/Athena R.C., in integrating the new structure selection algorithm to the PRESEMT prototype and on providing the translation results for the MOSES-based SMT system.

## References

Peter F. Brown, John Cocke, Stephen A. Della Pietra, Vincent J. Della Pietra, Frederick Jelinek, Robert L. Mercer, P. Roossin. 1988. A statistical approach to language translation. Proceedings of *COLING'88* Conference, Vol. 1, pp. 71–76.

Michael Denkowski and Alon Lavie. 2011. Meteor 1.3: Automatic Metric for Reliable Optimization and Evaluation of Machine Translation Systems, Proc. of the 6th Workshop on Statistical Machine Translation, Edinburgh, Scotland, UK, July 30–31, pp. 85–91.

John Hutchins. 2005. Example-Based Machine Translation: a Review and Commentary. Machine Translation, Vol. 19, pp.197-211.

Harry Mairson. 1992. The Stable Marriage Problem. The Brandeis Review, Vol.12, No.1. Available at: http://www.cs.columbia.edu/~evs/intro/stable/write up.html

Cory S. Myers, Lawrence R. Rabiner, and Aaron E. Rosenberg. 1980. Performance tradeoffs in dynamic time warping algorithms for isolated word recognition, IEEE Transactions on Acoustics, Speech, and Signal Processing, vol. 28, no. 6, pp. 623-635.

Philipp Koehn. 2010. Statistical machine translation. Cambridge University Press, Cambridge, UK [ISBN: 978-0-521-87415-1].

Uri Lerner, and Slav Petrov. 2013. Source-Side Classifier Preordering for Machine Translation. In Proceedings of EMNLP-2013 Conference, Seattle, USA, October 2013, pp.513-523.

Makoto Nagao. 1984. A framework of a mechanical translation between Japanese and English by analogy principle. Artificial and human intelligence: edited review papers presented at the international NATO Symposium, October 1981, Lyons, France; A. Elithorn and R. Banerji (eds.), Amsterdam: North Holland, pp. 173-180.

NIST. 2002. Automatic Evaluation of Machine Translation Quality Using n-gram Co-occurrences Statistics (Report). Available at: http://www.itl.nist.gov/iad/mig/tests/mt/doc/ngram-study.pdf

Kishore Papineni, Salim Roukos, Todd Ward and Wei-Jing Zhu. 2002. BLEU: A Method for Automatic Evaluation of Machine Translation. Proceedings of the 40th Annual Meeting of the Association for Computational Linguistics, Philadelphia, U.S.A., pp. 311-318.

Helmut Schmid. 1995. Improvements in Part-of-Speech Tagging with an Application to German. *Proceedings of the ACL SIGDAT-Workshop*. Dublin, Ireland.

Temple F. Smith, Michael S. Waterman. 1981. Identification of Common Molecular Subsequences. Journal of Molecular Biology, Vol.147, pp.195–197.

Matthew Snover, Bonnie Dorr, Richard Schwartz, Linnea Micciulla and John Makhoul. 2006. A Study of Translation Edit Rate with Targeted Human Annotation. Proceedings of the 7th AMTA Conference, Cambridge, MA, USA, pp.223-231.

Sokratis Sofianopoulos, Marina Vassiliou, and George Tambouratzis. 2012. Implementing a language-independent MT methodology. Proceedings of the First Workshop on Multilingual Modeling, held within the ACL-2012 Conference, Jeju, Republic of Korea, 13 July, pp.1-10.

Sara Stymne. 2012. Clustered Word Classes for Preordering in Statistical Machine Translation Proceedings of the 13th EACL Conference, April 23-27, Avignon, France, pp.28-34.

George Tambouratzis. 2014. Conditional Random Fields versus template-matching in MT phrasing tasks involving sparse training data. Pattern Recognition Letters, Vol. 53, pp.44-52.

George Tambouratzis, Sokratis Sofianopoulos, and Marina Vassiliou. 2014. Expanding the Language model in a low-resource hybrid MT system. In Proceedings of the SSST-8 Workshop, held within EMNLP-2014, 25 October 2014, Doha, Qatar, pp. 57-66.

# Passive and Pervasive Use of a Bilingual Dictionary in Statistical Machine Translation

**Liling Tan**[1], **Josef van Genabith**[1] **and Francis Bond**[2]
Universität des Saarland[1] / Campus, Saarbrücken, Germany
Nanyang Technological University[2] / 14 Nanyang Drive, Singapore
liling.tan@uni-saarland.de, josef.van_genabith@dfki.de,
bond@ieee.org

### Abstract

There are two primary approaches to the use bilingual dictionary in statistical machine translation: (i) the passive approach of appending the parallel training data with a bilingual dictionary and (ii) the pervasive approach of enforcing translation as per the dictionary entries when decoding. Previous studies have shown that both approaches provide external lexical knowledge to statistical machine translation thus improving translation quality. We empirically investigate the effects of both approaches on the same dataset and provide further insights on how lexical information can be reinforced in statistical machine translation.

## 1 Introduction

Statistical Machine Translation (SMT) obtains the best translation, $e_{best}$, by maximizing the conditional probability of the foreign sentence given the source sentence, $p(\mathrm{f}|\mathrm{e})$, and the a priori probability of the translation, $p_{LM}(\mathrm{e})$ (Brown, 1993).

$$\begin{aligned} e_{best} &= \underset{e}{\operatorname{argmax}} \quad p(e|f) \\ &= \underset{e}{\operatorname{argmax}} \quad p(f|e) \quad p_{LM}(e) \end{aligned}$$

State-of-art SMT systems rely on (i) large bilingual corpora to train the translation model $p(\mathrm{f}|\mathrm{e})$ and (ii) monolingual corpora to build the language model, $p_{LM}(\mathrm{e})$.

One approach to improve the translation model is to extend the parallel data with a bilingual dictionary prior to training the model. The primary motivation to use additional lexical information for domain adaptation to overcome the out-of-vocabulary words during decoding (Koehn and Schroeder, 2007; Meng et al. 2014; Wu et al. 2008). Alternatively, adding in-domain lexicon to parallel data has also shown to improve SMT. The intuition is that by adding extra counts of bilingual lexical entries, the word alignment accuracy improves, resulting in a better translation model (Skadins et al. 2013; Tan and Pal, 2014; Tan and Bond, 2014).

Another approach to use a bilingual dictionary is to hijack the decoding process and force word/phrase translations as per the dictionary entries. Previous researches used this approach to explore various improvements in industrial and academic translation experiments. For instance, Tezcan and Vandeghinste (2011) injected a bilingual dictionary in the SMT decoding process and integrated it with Computer Assisted Translation (CAT) environment to translate documents in the technical domain. They showed that using a dictionary in decoding improves machine translation output and reduces post-editing time of human translators. Carpuat (2009) experimented with translating sentences in discourse context by using a discourse specific dictionary annotations to resolve lexical ambiguities and showed that this can potentially improve translation quality.

In this paper, we investigate the improvements made by both approaches to use a bilingual dictionary in SMT. We refer to the first approach of extending the parallel data with dictionary as the ***passive*** use and the latter approach of hijacking the decoding process as the ***pervasive*** use of dictionary in statistical machine translation.

Different from the normal use of a dictionary for the purpose of domain adaptation where normally, a domain-specific lexicon is appended to a translation model trained on generic texts, we are investigating the use of an in-domain dictionary in statistical machine translation.

More specifically, we seek to understand how much improvement can be made by skewing the lexical information towards the passive and pervasive use of the dictionary in statistical machine



*Proceedings of the ACL 2015 Fourth Workshop on Hybrid Approaches to Translation (HyTra)*, pages 30–34,
Beijing, China, July 31, 2015. 

translation.

## 2 Passive vs Pervasive Use of Dictionary

We view both the passive and the pervasive use of a dictionary in statistical machine translation as a type of ***lexically constrained statistical hybrid MT*** where in the passive use, the dictionary acts a a supplementary set of bi-lexical rules affecting word and phrase alignments and the resulting translation model and in the pervasive use, the dictionary constraints the decoding search space enforcing translations as per the dictionary entries.

To examine the ***passive use*** of a dictionary, we explore the effects of adding the lexicon *n* number of times to the training data until the performance of the machine translation degrades.

For the ***pervasive use*** of a dictionary, we assign a uniform translation probability to possible translations of the source phrase. For instance, according to the dictionary, the English term "abnormal hemoglobin" could be translated to 異常ヘモグロビン or 異常血色素, we assign the translation probability of 0.5 to both Japanese translations, i.e. *p*(異常ヘモグロビン | *abnormal hemoglobin*) = *p*(異常血色素 | *abnormal hemoglobin*) = 0.5. If there is only one translation for a term in the dictionary, we force a translation from the dictionary by assigning the translation probability 1.0 to the translation.

One issue with the pervasive use of dictionary translations is the problem of compound phrases in the test sentence that are made up of ***component phrases*** in the dictionary. For instance, when decoding the sentence, "*Here was developed a phase shift magnetic sensor system composed of two sets of coils , amplifiers , and phase shifts for sensing and output .*", we fetch the following entries from the dictionary to translate the underlined multi-word term:

- *magnetic* =磁気
- *sensor* = センサ, センサー, 感知器, 感知部, 感応素子, 検出変換器, 変換素子, 受感部, 感覚器, センサー
- *system* = 組織体制, 制度, 子系, 系列, システム, 体系, 方式, 系統, 秩序, 体制, 組織, 一方式
- *magnetic sensor* = 磁気センサ
- *sensor system* = センサシステム, センサ系, センサーシステム

In such a situation, where the dictionary does not provide a translation for the complete multi-word string, we set the preference for the dictionary entry with the longest length in the direction from left to right and select "*magnetic sensor*" + "*system*" entries for forced translation.[1]

Finally, we investigate the effects of using the bilingual dictionary both passively and pervasively by appending the dictionary before training and hijacking the decoding by forcing translations using the same dictionary.

## 3 Experimental Setup

We experimented the passive and pervasive uses of dictionary in SMT using the Japanese-English dataset provided in the Workshop for Asian Translation (Toshiaki et al. 2014). We used the Asian Scientific Paper Excerpt Corpus (ASPEC) as the training corpus used in the experiments. The ASPEC corpus consists of 3 million parallel sentences extracted from Japanese-English scientific abstracts from Japan's Largest Electronic Journal Platform for Academic Societies (J-STAGE). In our experiments we follow the setup of the WAT shared task with 1800 development and test sentences each from the ASPEC corpus.

We use the Japanese-English (JA-EN) translation dictionaries (JICST, 2004) from the Japan Science and Technology Corporation. It contains 800,000 entries[2] for technical terms extracted from scientific and technological documents. Both the parallel data and the bilingual dictionary are tokenized with the `MeCab` segmenter (Kudo et al. 2004).

| Dataset | Japanese | English |
|---|---|---|
| `Train` | 86M | 78M |
| `Dev.` | 47K | 44K |
| `Test` | 47K | 44K |
| `Dict.` | 2.1M | 1.7M |

Table 1: Size of Training (`Train`), Development (`Dev.`) and Test (`Test`) Dataset from the ASPEC Corpus and JICST Dictionary (`Dict.`).

Table 1 presents the number of tokens in the ASPEC corpus and the JICST dictionary. On average 3-4 dictionary entries are found for each sentence

[1]Code to automatically convert sentences into XML-input with pervasive dictionary translations for the Moses toolkit is available at `http://tinyurl.com/pervasive-py`.

[2]2.1M JA and 1.7M EN tokens

in the WAT development set.

For all experiments we used the phrase-based SMT implemented in the Moses toolkit (Koehn et al, 2007) with the following experimental settings:

- `MGIZA++` implementation of IBM word alignment model 4 with grow-diagonal-final-and heuristics for word alignment and phrase-extraction (Och and Ney, 2003; Koehn et al., 2003; Gao and Vogel, 2008)
- Bi-directional lexicalized reordering model that considers monotone, swap and discontinuous orientations (Koehn et al., 2005 and Galley and Manning, 2008)
- Language modeling is trained using `KenLM` with maximum phrase length of 5 with Kneser-Ney smoothing (Heafield, 2011; Kneser and Ney, 1995)
- Minimum Error Rate Training (MERT) (Och, 2003) to tune the decoding parameters.
- For English translations, we trained a truecasing model to keep/reduce tokens' capitalization to their statistical canonical form (Wang et al., 2006; Lita et al., 2003) and we recased the translation output after the decoding process

Addtionally, we applied the following methods to optimize the phrase-based translation model for efficiency:

- To reduce the size of the language model and the speed of querying the model when decoding, we used the binarized trie-based quantized language model provided in `KenLM` (Heafield et al. 2013, Whittaker and Raj, 2001)
- To minimize the computing load on the translation model, we compressed the phrase-table and lexical reordering model using the `cmph` tool (Junczys-Dowmunt, 2012)

For the passive use of the dictionary, we simply appended the dictionary to the training data before the alignment and training process. For the pervasive use of the dictionary, we used the `xml-input` function in the Moses toolkit to force lexical knowledge in the decoding process[3].

[3]http://www.statmt.org/moses/?n=Advanced.Hybrid#ntoc1

## 4 Results

Table 2 presents the BLEU scores of the Japanese to English (JA-EN) translation outputs from the phrase-based SMT system on the WAT test set. The leftmost columns indicate the number of times a dictionary is appended to the parallel training data (*Baseline* = 0 times, *Passive x1* = 1 time). The rightmost columns present the results from both the passive and pervasive use of dictionary translations, with exception to the top-right cell which shows the baseline result of the pervasive dictionary usage without appending any dictionary.

| | - Pervasive | + Pervasive |
|---|---|---|
| Baseline | 16.75 | 16.87 |
| Passive x1 | 16.83 | 17.30** |
| Passive x2 | **17.31**** | 16.87 |
| Passive x3 | 17.26* | 17.06 |
| Passive x4 | 17.14* | **17.38**** |
| Passive x5 | 16.82 | 17.29** |

Table 2: BLEU Scores for Passive and Pervasive Use of the Dictionary in SMT (Japanese to English)

By repeatedly appending the dictionary to the parallel data, the BLEU scores significantly[4] improves from 16.75 to 17.31. Although the system's performance degrades when adding the dictionary passively thrice, the score remains significantly better than baseline. The pervasive use of the dictionary improves the baseline without the passive of the dictionary. The best performance is achieved when the dictionary is passively added four times with the pervasive use of the dictionary during decoding.

The fluctuations in improvement from coupling the passive and pervasive use of an in-domain dictionary give no indication of how both approaches should be used in tandem. However, using either or both the approaches improves the translation quality of the baseline system.

Table 3 presents the BLEU scores of the English to Japanese (EN-JA) translation outputs from the phrase-based SMT system on the WAT test set. Similarly, the passive use of dictionary outperforms the baseline but the pervasive use of dictionary consistently reported worse BLEU scores significantly.

Different from the JA-EN translation the pervasive use of dictionary consistently performs worse

[4]*: p-value<0.1, **: p-value<0.001

| | - Pervasive | + Pervasive |
|---|---|---|
| Baseline | 23.91 | 23.14** |
| Passive +1 | 24.12* | 23.13** |
| Passive +2 | 23.79 | 22.86** |
| Passive +3 | **24.14*** | **23.29**** |
| Passive +4 | 24.13* | 23.16** |
| Passive +5 | 23.67 | 22.71** |

Table 3: BLEU Scores for Passive and Pervasive Use of Dictionary in SMT (English to Japanese)

than the baseline. Upon random manual checking of the MT output, there are many instances where the technical/scientific term in the dictionary is translated correctly with only the passive use of the dictionary. However, it unclear whether the overall quality of the translations have degraded from the pervasive use of the dictionary given the slight, though significant, decrease in BLEU scores.

## 5 Conclusion

Empirically, both passive and pervasive use of a in-domain dictionary to extend statistical machine translation models with lexical knowledge modestly improve translation quality.

Interestingly, the fact that adding the in-domain dictionary information multiple times to the training data improves MT suggests that there may be a critical probability mass that a lexicon can impact the word and phrasal alignments in a corpus. This may provide insight on optimizing the weights of the salient in-domain phrases in the phrase table.

Although the pervasive use of dictionary information provides minimal or no improvements to the BLEU scores in our experiments, it remains relevant in industrial machine translation where terminological standardization is crucial in ensuring consistent translations of technical manuals or legal texts where incorrect use of terminology may have legal consequences (Porsiel, 2011).

The reported BLEU improvements from the passive information use of dictionary are good indication of improved machine translation quality but BLEU scores deterioration in the pervasive use only indicates that the output is not the same as the reference translation. Further manual evaluation is necessary to verify the poor performance of the pervasive use of dictionary information in machine translation.

## Acknowledgments

The research leading to these results has received funding from the People Programme (Marie Curie Actions) of the European Union's Seventh Framework Programme FP7/2007-2013/ under REA grant agreement n ° 317471.

## References

Marine Carpuat. 2009. One translation per discourse. In *Proceedings of the Workshop on Semantic Evaluations: Recent Achievements and Future Directions*, pages 19–27.

Michel Galley and Christopher D Manning. 2008. A simple and effective hierarchical phrase reordering model. In *Proceedings of the Conference on Empirical Methods in Natural Language Processing*, pages 848–856.

Qin Gao and Stephan Vogel. 2008. Parallel implementations of word alignment tool. In *Software Engineering, Testing, and Quality Assurance for Natural Language Processing*, pages 49–57.

Kenneth Heafield, Ivan Pouzyrevsky, Jonathan H. Clark, and Philipp Koehn. 2013. Scalable modified kneser-ney language model estimation. In *Proceedings of the 51st Annual Meeting of the Association for Computational Linguistics (Volume 2: Short Papers)*, pages 690–696, Sofia, Bulgaria, August.

Kenneth Heafield. 2011. KenLM: faster and smaller language model queries. In *Proceedings of the EMNLP 2011 Sixth Workshop on Statistical Machine Translation*, pages 187–197, Edinburgh, Scotland, United Kingdom, July.

JICST, editor. 2004. *JICST Japanese-English translation dictionaries*. Japan Information Center of Science and Technology.

Marcin Junczys-Dowmunt. 2012. Phrasal rank-encoding: Exploiting phrase redundancy and translational relations for phrase table compression. *The Prague Bulletin of Mathematical Linguistics*, 98:63–74.

Reinhard Kneser and Hermann Ney. 1995. Improved backing-off for m-gram language modeling. In *Acoustics, Speech, and Signal Processing, 1995. ICASSP-95., 1995 International Conference on*, volume 1, pages 181–184. IEEE.

Philipp Koehn and Josh Schroeder. 2007. Experiments in domain adaptation for statistical machine translation. In *Proceedings of the Second Workshop on Statistical Machine Translation*, pages 224–227.

Philipp Koehn, Franz Josef Och, and Daniel Marcu. 2003. Statistical phrase-based translation. In *Proceedings of the 2003 Conference of the North*

*American Chapter of the Association for Computational Linguistics on Human Language Technology-Volume 1*, pages 48–54.

Philipp Koehn. 2005. Europarl: A parallel corpus for statistical machine translation. In *Proceedings of MT Summit, vol. 5, pp. 79-86.*

Lucian Vlad Lita, Abraham Ittycheriah, Salim Roukos, and Nanda Kambhatla. 2003. tRuEcasIng. In Erhard Hinrichs and Dan Roth, editors, *Proceedings of the 41st Annual Meeting of the Association for Computational Linguistics*, pages 152–159.

Fandong Meng, Deyi Xiong, Wenbin Jiang, and Qun Liu. 2014. Modeling term translation for document-informed machine translation. In *Proceedings of the 2014 Conference on Empirical Methods in Natural Language Processing (EMNLP)*, pages 546–556, Doha, Qatar, October.

Toshiaki Nakazawa, Hideya Mino, Isao Goto, Sadao Kurohashi, and Eiichiro Sumita. 2014. Overview of the 1st workshop on asian translation. In *Proceedings of the 1st Workshop on Asian Translation (WAT2014).*

Franz Josef Och and Hermann Ney. 2003. A systematic comparison of various statistical alignment models. *Computational linguistics*, 29(1):19–51.

Raivis Skadiņš, Mārcis Pinnis, Tatiana Gornostay, and Andrejs Vasiļjevs. 2013. Application of online terminology services in statistical machine translation. pages 281–286.

Liling Tan and Francis Bond. 2014. Manipulating input data in machine translation. In *Proceedings of the 1st Workshop on Asian Translation (WAT2014).*

Liling Tan and Santanu Pal. 2014. Manawi: Using multi-word expressions and named entities to improve machine translation. In *Proceedings of the Ninth Workshop on Statistical Machine Translation*, pages 201–206, Baltimore, Maryland, USA, June.

Arda Tezcan and Vincent Vandeghinste. 2011. Smt-cat integration in a technical domain: Handling xml markup using pre & post-processing methods. *Proceedings of EAMT 2011.*

Yulia Tsvetkov and Shuly Wintner. 2012. Extraction of multi-word expressions from small parallel corpora. *Natural Language Engineering*, 18(04):549–573.

Stephan Vogel and Christian Monson. 2004. Augmenting manual dictionaries for statistical machine translation systems. In *Proceedings of the Fourth International Conference on Language Resources and Evaluation (LREC'04).*

Wei Wang, Kevin Knight, and Daniel Marcu. 2006. Capitalizing machine translation. In *Proceedings of the Human Language Technology Conference of the NAACL, Main Conference*, pages 1–8, New York City, USA, June. Association for Computational Linguistics.

Edward WD Whittaker and Bhiksha Raj. 2001. Quantization-based language model compression. In *Proceedings of INTERSPEECH*, pages 33–36.

Hua Wu, Haifeng Wang, and Chengqing Zong. 2008. Domain adaptation for statistical machine translation with domain dictionary and monolingual corpora. In *Proceedings of the 22nd International Conference on Computational Linguistics-Volume 1*, pages 993–1000.

# Automated Simultaneous Interpretation: Hints of a Cognitive Framework for Machine Translation

**Rafael E. Banchs**
Institute for Infocomm Research
1 Fusionopolis Way, #21-01, Singapore 138632
rembanchs@i2r.a-star.edu.sg

### Abstract

This discussion paper presents and analyses the main conceptual differences and similarities between the human task of simultaneous interpretation and the statistical approach to machine translation. A psycho-cognitive model of the simultaneous interpretation process is reviewed and compared with the phrase-based statistical machine translation approach. Some interesting differences are identified and their possible implications on machine translation methods are discussed. Finally, the most relevant research problems related to them are identified.

## 1. Introduction

Nowadays, translation has become an important element of daily life. Indeed, the emergence of modern information and communication technologies and the resulting globalization phenomenon are continuously boosting the need for translation services and applications. Within the context of professional translation, three different types of human translation tasks can be identified:

***Document translation***. This task refers to the situation in which the professional translator is required to generate a target-language-version of a given source document. In this kind of situations, full understanding of the source material is required and full generation of the target must be accomplished. In general, free translations are acceptable, no specific time constraints are imposed, and the best translation quality is expected.

***Consecutive interpretation***. This task refers to the situation in which the professional translator is required to mediate the communication between two persons that speaks different languages. The basic communication protocol in this case is based in a turn-taking strategy, in which interlocutors must speak one at a time when they are given the right to speak. In this kind of situations, full understanding of the source material is required and full generation of the target must be ideally accomplished, while a 'shared' time constrains exists.

***Simultaneous interpretation***. This task refers to the situation in which the professional translator is required to translate on-the-fly what other person is saying in a different language. In this case no turn-taking is allowed as the translator is expected to produce the translated speech while the main speaker continues speaking. In these situations, full understanding and full generation is not mandatory, as the interpreter must keep the main speaker's pace because 'concurrent' time constraints exist.

Current machine translation technologies have been theoretically and empirically designed under assumptions related to the first and second categories defined above. As far as we know, only few attempts have been done to apply machine translation to the specific problem of simultaneous interpretation. Indeed, previous research in this area can be traced back to the Vermobil[1] project, as well as to work from Kitano (1991) and Furuse and Iida (1996), who proposed the use of incremental translation. Later on, Mima *et al.* (1998) developed the idea of example-based incremental transfer.

The main objective of this discussion paper is to highlight the differences and similarities between the human task of simultaneous interpretation and statistical machine translation aiming at proposing

[1] https://en.wikipedia.org/wiki/Verbmobil



*Proceedings of the ACL 2015 Fourth Workshop on Hybrid Approaches to Translation (HyTra)*, pages 35–39,
Beijing, China, July 31, 2015. 

a research agenda for problems related to automated simultaneous interpretation. The rest of this discussion paper is structured as follows. First, in section 2, a recently proposed psycho-cognitive model of human simultaneous interpretation is presented along with its possible implications on machine translation. Then, in section 3, a cognitive framework for machine translation based on the described psycho-cognitive model is proposed.

## 2. Comparative Analysis

Although the translation process might slightly vary from person to person depending on a wide variety of factors, according to recently proposed psychological models of memory and attention (Padilla-Benítez and Bajo 1998), during a simultaneous interpretation task five different subtasks are conducted by the human brain: listening, segmentation, translation, reordering, and utterance production.

### 2.1 A Model of Simultaneous Interpretation

According to the aforementioned process, a human interpreter segments the input utterance into meaning units, which constitute basic semantic units that can be represented and manipulated at the cognitive level (Oleron and Nanpon 1965). An interesting, and also curious, fact about these meaning units is that the average human brain is able to process $7 \pm 2$ of such units at a time (Miller 1956). This seems to be indicating some sort of cognitive buffer size which happens to be independent of the language.

In parallel to the segmentation process, each meaning unit is translated by taking into account the surrounding $7 \pm 2$ unit context, and after having translated several units reordering and post-edition procedures are performed; producing, in this way, the output utterance. All these parallel processes are continuously operating while the input utterance is being received and the output utterance is being emitted; this last one with a corresponding latency of some few words.

### 2.2 Main Differences with SMT

Based on the information above, some important observations can be derived.

First, notice that the processes of translation and reordering are conducted sequentially, in the sense that reordering and utterance production are conducted after some meaning units have been translated. So, differently from the SMT framework, in which translation and reordering are performed simultaneously during decoding; in the human interpretation case, reordering is performed after translation. This means that reordering decisions do not affect unit selection.

Second, unit selection is made by taking into account a $7 \pm 2$ meaning unit context, which includes both preceding and subsequent semantic information. As each meaning unit is composed of several words, the considered contexts in this case are larger than the ones considered in SMT, as well as they span over subsequent words.

No complex search strategy seems to be applied by the human interpreters. Indeed, the search strategy seems to be much simpler than in the case of SMT decoding. By decomposing the decoding task into two separated processes: translation and reordering, a simpler search strategy can be utilized.

### 2.3 Automated Simultaneous Interpretation

The three basic observations described above have very important implications on the way state-of-the-art SMT operates, and on the possible avenues of research for adapting this kind of systems to the specific task of simultaneous interpretation. These implications are described below.

The translation strategy is indeed very simple: a 1-to-1 mapping between meaning units which is context dependent. In the ideal case, the context and the source meaning unit must almost uniquely define the corresponding target meaning unit.

Although meaning units are not clearly defined by psychologists, they can be thought of as a set of optimal units for information representation and transference, which admit translation. According to this, meaning units should not be either generated or deleted during translation (i.e. for a given input, the corresponding translation must have the same number of meaning units).

Although reordering continues to be a NP-complete problem, the search space can be strongly reduced as meaning unit mapping should be able to produce a much reduced set of candidate translation units. In the ideal scenario, stacks of size 1 would be produced and reordering can be reduced to a simple permutation strategy of meaning units rather than words.

Source context plays a very important role in the human simultaneous interpretation framework, and human translation in general. This means that both semantics and pragmatics have a preponderant role in the process of translation production, which moves a step ahead from current state-of-the-art technologies that make a very limited use of source context information.

Based on these important implications and the corresponding observations they were derived from, in the following section, we will attempt to define a research agenda for the problem under consideration. In such a research agenda, we define the main challenges and subtasks that must be addressed for successfully applying current state-of-the-art machine translation technologies to the problem of automatic simultaneous interpretation.

## 3. A Cognitive Framework for SMT

By taking into account the psycho-cognitive model for simultaneous interpretation described in the previous section, we can propose a SMT framework for automated simultaneous interpretation. In such an approach, the following four basic subtasks must be considered:

***Segmentation***. This subtask is responsible for segmenting the input data stream into meaning units which admit translation. Such meaning units must be minimal in the sense that not subunits can be contained into them, and must be maximal in the sense that, given a semantic context, translatability for every unit is guaranteed.

***Translation or target unit selection***. This subtask is responsible for selecting (or generating) the most appropriate target meaning unit for translating each input meaning unit within the current block of data under consideration. Target unit selection must be done by taking into account both the source unit to be translated and its context.

***Reordering***. This subtask is responsible for generating appropriate reordering for target units. Notice that this kind of reordering accounts only for long reordering (chunk reordering), as short reordering (word reordering) has been already accounted for in the unit selection stage. Reordering decisions in this task must be mainly done based on target language information.

***Post-edition***. This subtask is responsible for concatenating the reordered target units. This subtask must deal with two specific types of problems: boundary overlapping, where consecutive units are to be merged by resolving possible word overlapping; and boundary gaps, where consecutive units are to be concatenated by filling-in possible gaps.

The proposed strategy allows for concurrently generating a target output stream while a source input stream is being received. The four aforementioned subtasks are to be pipelined so they sequentially process a given block of data. However, they are concurrently operating over a buffered stream of data. As a logical consequence of the pipeline, the overall system exhibits some latency, which must be in the range between 5 to 15 words if the automatic system is intended to mimic human simultaneous interpretation (Padilla-Benítez and Bajo 1998).

### 3.1 Source Input Segmentation

The main challenges of this subtask include the definition and operationalization of meaning units, as well as the definition of contextual boundaries. According to the previous discussion, a meaning unit must satisfy the following constraints:

***Informative***. The meaning unit must constitute a self-contained and elementary unit of information, which should be understandable within its context but without the need for specific informational elements from the surrounding units.

***Translatable***. The meaning unit must have an equivalent representation in the target language. If the complete source message is to be transmitted through the translation process, all individual source units must have a corresponding target unit. Source and target meaning units in a parallel sentence pair should admit one-to-one alignments.

***Minimal***. A meaning unit should not contain sub-units that are coherently both informative and translatable.

Although there is not a clear definition on what psychologists refer to as a meaning unit, the above described properties make it clear their utility as basic elements for information transmission and understanding. From these properties and the specific characteristics of the problem under consideration, a pragmatic definition for meaning units can be grounded on a translation optimality criterion, such as a unique segmentation which minimizes the translation effort and maximizes the translation quality.

Research work on this specific subtask must be supported by and would certainly benefit from recent research in the areas of collocation extraction, multiword expression identification, name entity recognition and shallow parsing.

A recent study (Williams et al. 2013) explored the task of meaning unit segmentation by human annotators in languages such as English and Chinese. The result of this study suggested that no optimal solution seems to exist for this problem. Although any random segmentation is definitively not acceptable, it seems to be some preferential but variable trends on how humans perform meaning unit segmentation.

### 3.2 Target Unit Selection

One of the most interesting observations derived from the psycho-cognitive model is that the translation of a given meaning unit seems to be uniquely determined by its surrounding context. This fact allows for a theoretical justification on decoupling the problem of unit selection from the problem of reordering (long reordering, actually), as the problem of target unit selection becomes independent from the target language structure, which can be dealt with afterwards by means of reordering strategies that should only use target language information. The main properties that are desirable for target unit selection according to the proposed methodology are as follows:

***Completeness***. One source meaning unit should be translated by means of one target meaning unit which conveys an equivalent amount and type of information.

***Unambiguousness***. The available context information must be used to resolve ambiguity problems at this stage. According to this, the possible options for a target meaning unit, given a source meaning unit, should be restricted to a very small set of equivalent meaning units.

Different from state-of-the-art SMT, in which a large number of possible translations are considered and filtered by means of frequency-based criterions, the main objective of the proposed target unit selection approach is to fully use the context information to resolve ambiguity and produce a restricted set of candidate units. This reduction of target unit candidates should guarantee a better overall lexical selection as well as reduce the computational complexity of the decoding process.

Research work on this specific subtask of target unit selection can be supported by and would certainly benefit from recent research in the areas of word sense disambiguation, distributional semantics, syntax-based machine translation, and cross-language information retrieval.

Significant effort on using source-context information to improve target unit selection has been reported during the last few years for both domain adaptation and lexical semantics (Carpuat and Wu 2005, España-Bonet et al. 2009, Haque et al. 2010, Banchs and Costa-jussà 2011)

### 3.3 Target Unit Reordering

Reordering is probably one of the most important challenges in SMT research, as well as it is the key factor responsible for decoding being an NP-complete problem (Zaslavskiy et al. 2009). The significant reduction of candidate hypothesis resulting from the use of source context information during target unit selection certainly reduces the computational burden for reordering. According to this, a more exhaustive search of the solution space can be afforded, which should also help improving the quality of the resulting translations.

Notice that, in this specific subtask, we are dealing with chunk-based reordering rather than word-based reordering. Indeed, word-reordering is assumed to be accounted for during the phase of target unit selection, in which each target meaning unit should already incorporate the corresponding word-reordering that is required to convey the desired meaning.

Valuable research related to this area includes lexicalized reordering as well as class-based reordering, dependency parsing and syntax based machine translation (Li et al. 2007, Nagata et al 2006, Zhang et al. 2007, Costa-jussa and Fonollosa 2006, Wang et al. 2007).

### 3.4 Output Post-Edition

The final subtask in our proposed framework has to do with the specific problem of merging the resulting sequence of output meaning units. After meaning unit selection and reordering, a simple concatenation strategy does not guarantee a fluid and grammatically correct output utterance.

Specific problems at the boundaries of the consecutive meaning units can be expected to occur, which can be basically grouped into two categories: boundary overlapping and boundary gaps. In this sense, the post-edition subtask can be thought of as a smoothing procedure for making the concatenation of consecutive meaning units more fluid and grammatical.

Research work on this specific subtask of output post-edition can be supported by and would certainly benefit from recent research in areas such as language modeling, syntactic- and semantic-based grammatical correction, and paraphrasing.

## 4. Conclusions

This paper discussed the main conceptual differences and similarities between the human task of simultaneous interpretation and the statistical approach to machine translation. A psycho-cognitive model of the simultaneous interpretation process was reviewed and compared with the statistical machine translation approach. Based on this, a research agenda for cognitive-based automated simultaneous interpretation has been discussed.

The most important application of automated simultaneous interpretation would be in the area of speech-to-speech translation; and more specifically in the case computer-mediated cross-language dialogue or discourse.

## References


Rafael E. Banchs and Marta R. Costa-jussa. 2011. A semantic feature for statistical machine translation. In Proceedings of the Fifth Workshop on Syntax, Semantics and Structure in Statistical Translation, SSST-5, pages 126–134.

Marine Carpuat and Dekai Wu. 2005. Word sense disambiguation vs. statistical machine translation. In-Proceedings of the 43rd Annual Meeting on Association for Computational Linguistics, ACL '05, pages 387–394, Stroudsburg, PA, USA.

Boxing Chen, Roland Kuhn, and George Foster. 2013. Vector space model for adaptation in statistical machine translation. In Proceedings of the 51st Annual Meeting of the Association for Computational Linguistics (Volume 1: Long Papers), pages 1285– 1293, Sofia, Bulgaria, August.

Marta R. Costa-jussà and José A. R. Fonollosa. (2006) Statistical machine reordering}. In Proceedings of the 2006 Conference on Empirical Methods in Natural Language Processing, p.70--76

Cristina España Bonet, Jesus Gimenez, and Lluıs Marquez. 2009. Discriminative phrase-based models for arabic machine translation. Transactions on Asian Language and Information Processing, 8(4):15:1–15:20, December.

Osamu Furuse and Hitoshi Iida. 1996. Incremental Translation Utilizing Constituent Boundary Patterns. In *Proceedings of Coling'96*, pages 544–549

Hiroaki Kitano. 1991. Φ DM-Dialog: An Experimental Speech-to-Speech Dialog Translation System. *Computer* 24(6):36–50.

C.H. Li, D. Zhang, M. Li, M. Zhou, M. Li, and Y. Guan. 2007. A probabilistic approach to syntax-based reordering for statistical machine translation. In Proc. of ACL, pages 720–727, June

George A. Miller. 1956. The Magical Number Seven, Plus or Minus Two: Some Limits on Our Capacity of Processing Information. The Psychological Review, Vol 63:81–97.

Hideki Mima, Hitoshi Iida and Osamu Furuse. 1998. Simultaneous interpretation utilizing example-based incremental transfer. In *Proceedings of the 36th Annual Meeting of the Association for Computational Linguistics*, pages 855–861

M. Nagata, K. Saito, K. Yamamoto, and K. Ohashi. 2006. A clustered global phrase reordering model for statistical machine translation. In Proc. of ACL, page 720

Pierre Oleron and Hubert Nanpon. 1965. Recherches sur la traduction simultan´ee. Journal de Psychologie Normale et Pathologique, 62(1):73–94.

Presentación Padilla Benítez and Teresa Bajo. 1998. Hacia un modelo de memoria y atención en interpretación simultanea. Quaderns. Revista de traduccio, 2:107–117.

C. Wang, M. Collins, and P. Koehn. 2007. Chinese syntactic reordering for statistical machine translation. In Proc. of EMNLP, pages 737–745.

Jennifer Williams, Rafael E. Banchs and Haizhou Li. 2013. Meaning unit segmentation in English and Chinese: a new approach to discourse phenomena. In Proceedings of Workshop on Discourse in Machine Translation (DiscoMT), ACL 2013.

Mikhail Zaslavskiy, Marc Dymetman and Nicola Cancedda. 2009. Phrase-Based Statistical Machine Translation as a Travelling Salesman Problem. In Proceedings of the 47th Annual Meeting of the ACL and the 4th IJCNLP of the AFNLP, pages 333–341, Suntec, Singapore.

Y. Zhang, R. Zens, and H. Ney. 2007. Improved chunklevel reordering for statistical machine translation. In Proc. of IWSLT, pages 21–28, Trento, Italy, October.

# A fuzzier approach to machine translation evaluation: A pilot study on post-editing productivity and automated metrics in commercial settings

**Carla Parra Escartín**
Hermes Traducciones
C/ Cólquide 6, portal 2, 3.º I
28230 Las Rozas, Madrid, Spain
carla.parra@hermestrans.com

**Manuel Arcedillo**
Hermes Traducciones
C/ Cólquide 6, portal 2, 3.º I
28230 Las Rozas, Madrid, Spain
manuel.arcedillo@hermestrans.com

## Abstract

Machine Translation (MT) quality is typically assessed using automatic evaluation metrics such as BLEU and TER. Despite being generally used in the industry for evaluating the usefulness of Translation Memory (TM) matches based on text similarity, fuzzy match values are not as widely used for this purpose in MT evaluation. We designed an experiment to test if this fuzzy score applied to MT output stands up against traditional methods of MT evaluation. The results obtained seem to confirm that this metric performs at least as well as traditional methods for MT evaluation.

## 1 Introduction

In recent years, Machine Translation Post-Editing (MTPE) has been introduced in real translation workflows as part of the production process. MTPE is used to reduce production costs and increase the productivity of professional translators. This productivity gain is usually reflected in translation rate discounts. However, the question of how to assess Machine Translation (MT) output in order to determine a fair compensation for the post-editor is still open.

Shortcomings of traditional metrics, such as BLEU (Papineni et al., 2001) and TER (Snover et al., 2006), when applied to MTPE include unclear correlation with productivity gains, technical difficulties for their estimation by general users and lack of intuitiveness. A more common metric already used in translation tasks for evaluating text similarity is the Translation Memory (TM) fuzzy match score. Based on the fuzzy score analysis, rate discounts due to TM leverage are then applied. We designed an experiment to test if this fuzzy score applied to MT output stands up against traditional methods of MT evaluation.

The remainder of this paper is structured as follows: Section 2 presents the rationale behind the experiment. Section 3 explains the pilot experiment itself. Section 4 reports the results obtained and what they have revealed, and finally Section 5 summarizes our work and discusses possible paths to explore in the light of our findings.

## 2 Rationale

As far as MT evaluation is concerned, a well-established evaluation metric is BLEU, although it has also received criticism (Koehn, 2010). It is usually considered that BLEU scores above 30 reflect understandable translations, while scores over 50 are considered good and fluent translations (Lavie, 2010). However, the usefulness of "understandable" translations for MTPE is questionable. Contrary to other MT applications, post-editors do not depend on MT to understand the meaning of a foreign-language sentence. Instead, they expect to re-use the largest possible text chunks to meet their client's requirements, regardless of the meaning or fluency conveyed by the raw MT output. This criticism also holds true for human annotations on Adequacy and Fluency[1].

Other metrics more focused in post-editing effort have been developed, such as TER. However, how should one interpret an improvement in BLEU score from 45 to 50 in terms of productivity? Likewise, does a TER value of 35 deserve any kind of discount? Most likely, the vast majority of translators would

[1] For details of these scores see, for example, the TAUS adequacy and fluency guidelines at `https://www.taus.net/`.



*Proceedings of the ACL 2015 Fourth Workshop on Hybrid Approaches to Translation (HyTra)*, pages 40–45, Beijing, China, July 31, 2015. ©2015 Association for Computational Linguistics

be unable to answer these questions and yet they would probably instantly acknowledge that fuzzy text similarities of 60% are not worth editing, while they would be happy to accept discounts for 80% fuzzy scores based on an analogy with TM matches. Organizations such as TAUS have already proposed alternative models which use fuzzy matches for MT evaluation, such as the "MT Reversed analysis".[2]

In order to compare alternative measures based on fuzzy matches with BLEU and TER scores, we designed an experiment involving both MTPE and translating from scratch in a real-life translation scenario. It is worth noting that the exact algorithm used by each Computer Assisted Translation (CAT) tool for computing the fuzzy score is unknown[3]. In this paper, we use the Sørensen-Dice coefficient (Sørensen, 1948; Dice, 1945) for fuzzy match scores, unless otherwise specified.

## 3 Pilot experiment settings

Following similar works (Federico et al., 2012), the experiment aimed to replicate a real production environment. Two in-house translators were asked to translate the same file from English into Spanish using one of their most common translation tools (memoQ[4]). This tool was chosen because of its feature for recording time spent in each segment. Other tools which also record this value and other useful segment-level indicators, such as keystrokes[5], or MTPE effort[6], were discarded due to them not being part of the everyday resources of the translators involved in the experiment. Translators were only allowed to use the TM, the terminology database and the MT output included in the translation package. Other memoQ's productivity enhancing features were disabled (especially, predictive text, sub-segment leverage and automatic fixing of fuzzy matches) to allow better comparisons with translation environments which may not offer similar features.

### 3.1 Text selection

The file to be translated had to meet the following requirements:

1. Belong to a real translation request.
2. Originate from a client for which our company owned a customized MT engine.
3. Have a word volume capable of engaging translators for several hours.
4. Include significant word counts for each TM match band (i.e., exact matches, fuzzy matches and no-match segments[7]).

The original source text selected contained over 8,000 words and was part of a software user guide. All repetitions and internal leverage segments were filtered out to avoid skewing due to the inferior typing and cognitive effort required to translate the second of two similar segments. During this text selection phase, we studied the word counts available for all past projects of this client, which were already generated using a different tool (SDL Trados Studio[8]) than the one finally used in the experiment (memoQ). Table 1 shows the word counts of our text according to both tools.

| | memoQ | | Trados Studio | |
|---|---|---|---|---|
| **TM match** | **Words** | **Seg.** | **Words** | **Seg.** |
| 100% | 1226 | 94 | 1243 | 95 |
| 95-99% | 231 | 21 | 1044 | 55 |
| 85-94% | 1062 | 48 | 747 | 43 |
| 75-84% | 696 | 42 | 608 | 42 |
| No Match | 3804 | 263 | 3388 | 233 |
| **Total** | **7019** | **468** | **7030** | **468** |

Table 1: Final word counts.

As Table 1 shows, CAT tools may differ greatly in the word counts and fuzzy match distribution. As Studio showed significant word volumes for every band, the file used for the test seemed appropriate. However, when using memoQ one of the fuzzy match bands (95-99%) ended up with significantly less words than the other bands. At the same time, there was an increase in no-match segments. This provided a more solid sample

[2]See the pricing MTPE guidelines at https://www.taus.net.

[3]It is believed that most are based on some adjustment of Levenshtein's edit distance (Levenshtein, 1965).

[4]The version used was memoQ 2015 build 3.

[5]For example, PET (Aziz et al., 2012) and iOmegaT (Moran et al., 2014).

[6]For example, MateCat (Federico et al., 2012).

[7]In general, any TM fuzzy match below 75% is considered a no-match segment due to the general acceptance that such leverage does not yield any productivity increase.

[8]The version used was SDL Trados Studio 2014 SP1.

for comparing MTPE and translation throughputs, increasing the count to 3804 words, half of which were randomly selected for MTPE using the test set generator included in the m4loc package[9]. Table 2 shows word counts after this division.

| Origin | Words | Segments |
|---|---|---|
| No Match (MTPE) | 1890 | 131 |
| No Match (Translation) | 1914 | 132 |
| **Total** | **3804** | **468** |

Table 2: No-match word count distribution after random division.

### 3.2 MT engine

The system used to generate the MT output was Systran's[10] RBMT engine. This is the system normally used in our company for post-editing machine translated texts from this client. It can be considered a mature engine, since at the time of the experiment it had been subject to ongoing in-house customization for over three years via dictionary entries, software settings, and pre- and post-editing scripts, as well as having a consistent record for productivity enhancement. Although Systran includes a Statistical Machine Translation (SMT) component, this was not used in our experiment because in previous tests it produced a less adequate MT output for MTPE.

### 3.3 Human translators

Both translators involved had five years' experience in translation. However, Translator 2 also had three years' experience in MTPE and had been involved in previous projects of this client. Translator 1 did not have any experience either in MTPE or with the client's texts. They were assigned a hand-off package which included all necessary files and settings for the experiment. They were asked to translate the file included in the package performing all necessary edits in the MT output and TM matches to achieve the standard full quality expected by the client.

## 4 Results and discussion

Once the translation and MTPE task was delivered by both translators, we analyzed their output using different metrics:

1. **Words per hour**: Amount of words translated/post-edited per hour, according to memoQ's word count and time tracking feature.
2. **Fuzzy match**: Based on the Sørensen-Dice coefficient, this metric is a statistic used to compare the similarity of two samples. We used the Okapi Rainbow library[11]. The comparison is based in 3-grams.
3. **BLEU**: Widely used for MT evaluation. It relies on n-gram overlapping.
4. **TER**: Another widely used metric, based on the number of edits required to make the MT output match a reference.
5. **Productivity gain**: Based on the number of words translated/post-edited per hour, we estimated the productivity gain for each band when compared to unaided translation throughput.

For the metrics involving a comparison, we compared the TM match suggestion or MT raw output against the final delivered text by the translators. The results of our evaluation are reported in Table 3.

| | W/h | Fuzzy | BLEU | TER | Prod. gain % |
|---|---|---|---|---|---|
| *Trans. 1* | | | | | |
| **100%** | 1542 | 97.50 | 91.96 | 4.64 | 65.20 |
| **95-99%** | 963 | 92.43 | 87.91 | 6.91 | 3.14 |
| **85-94%** | 1158 | 90.92 | 80.19 | 13.02 | 24.12 |
| **75-84%** | 1120 | 87.93 | 73.94 | 19.08 | 20.03 |
| **PE** | 910 | 88.53 | 69.57 | 18.89 | -2.46 |
| **TRA** | 933 | - | - | - | - |
| *Trans. 2* | | | | | |
| **100%** | 2923 | 97.91 | 92.38 | 3.99 | 121.61 |
| **95-99%** | 2625 | 92.76 | 89.35 | 6.37 | 99.05 |
| **85-94%** | 2237 | 91.19 | 81.00 | 12.69 | 69.61 |
| **75-84%** | 1585 | 85.21 | 71.98 | 21.03 | 20.17 |
| **PE** | 1728 | 87.74 | 66.37 | 20.98 | 31.00 |
| **TRA** | 1319 | - | - | - | - |

Table 3: Results obtained for both translators.

Both translators had unusually high throughputs for MTPE and unaided translation, especially when compared to the standard reference of 313-375 words per hour (2500-3000 words per day). Taking this as reference, Translator 1 would have experienced more than 140% productivity increase, while Translator 2 would have translated at least 350% faster. However, despite this high MTPE speed, Translator 1 did not experience

[9] https://code.google.com/p/m4loc/

[10] Systran 7 Premium Translator was used. No language model was applied.

[11] http://okapi.opentag.com/

any productivity gain (quite the contrary), while Translator 2 saw a productivity increase of "just" 31%. This may point out that the faster texts to translate are also the fastest to post-edit. Thus the importance of having an unaided translation reference for each sample instead of relying on standard values (Federico et al., 2012).

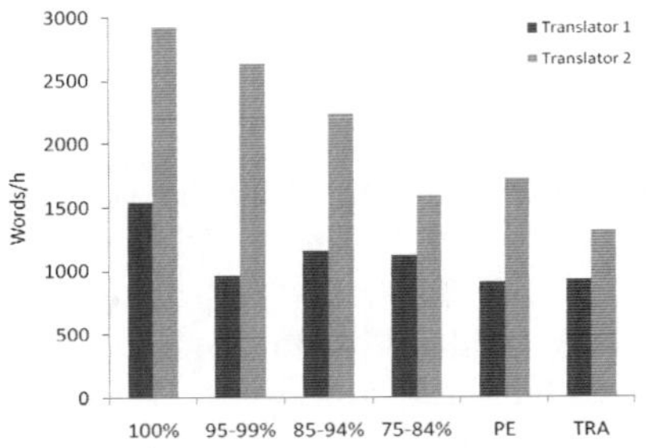


Figure 1: Productivity in words per hour of both translators.

The difference between the MT benefit for both translators might be due to the little MTPE experience of Translator 1. Furthermore, Translator 2 was already familiarized with the texts of this client, while it was the first time Translator 1 worked with them. Presumably, Translator 1 had to spend more time acquiring the client's preferred terminology and performing TM concordance lookups to achieve consistency with previously translated content. This seems to have negated part of the benefits of fuzzy matching and MT output leverage (see the flatness of Translator 1's throughputs for fuzzy, MTPE and translation bands in Figure 1). Translator 2 does show a distinct throughput for each category.

Another possible explanation for Translator 1's performance would be that the quality of the raw MT output is low. However, Translator 2's productivity gains and comparison with past projects' performance contradict this. We therefore concluded that the most probable explanation to the difference in terms of productivity might be due to the MTPE experience of both translators. In fact, studies about impact of translator's experience agree that more experienced translators do MTPE faster (Guerberof Arenas, 2009), although they do not usually distinguish between experience in translation and experience in MTPE.

Figures 2 and 3 plot the productivity for each band against the different evaluation measures discussed for Translator 1 and 2, respectively. TER has been inverted for a more direct comparison.

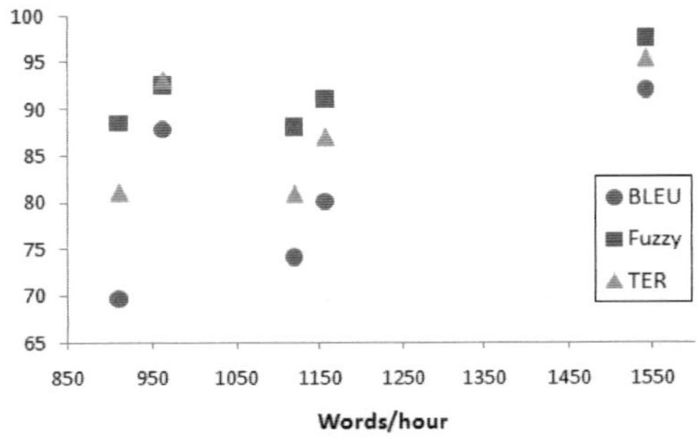


Figure 2: Productivity vs. automated measures for Translator 1.

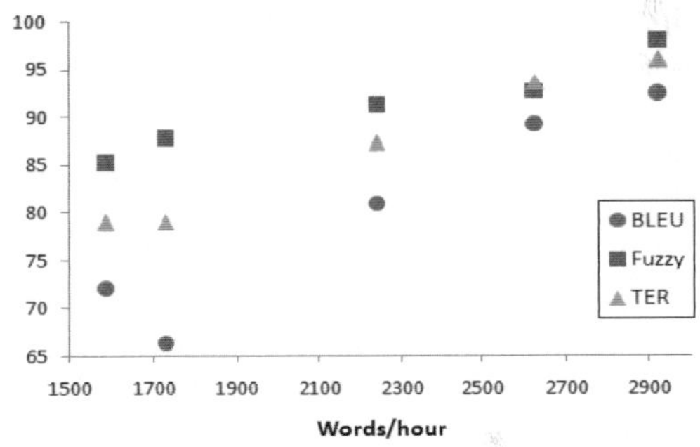


Figure 3: Productivity vs. automated measures for Translator 2.

It is remarkable that Translator 2's MTPE throughput was even higher than the one for the lowest fuzzy match band. According to BLEU (66.37 vs. 71.98), the situation should have been the opposite, while according to TER both throughputs should have been more or less the same (20.98 vs. 21.03). The fuzzy match value (87.74 vs. 85.21) is the only one from the chosen set of metrics to reflect the higher throughput of the MTPE sample over the 75-84% band.

Despite this fact, all three metrics showed a strong correlation with productivity for Translator 2, while the fuzzy score had the strongest correlation for Translator 1 (see Table 4). Based on the results obtained, the fuzzy score could be used in MTPE scenarios as a valid alternative metric for evaluating MT output.

Despite not being used often in research, we have found out that it could give a good insight on the translation quality of MT output, as it performs as good as or even better than the other metrics evaluated. At the same time, as it is a well-established metric in translation business, it might be easier for translators to understand and assess MTPE tasks.

| | $r_{fuzzy}$ | $r_{BLEU}$ | $r_{TER}$ |
|---|---|---|---|
| **Trans. 1** | 0.785 | 0.639 | 0.568 |
| **Trans. 2** | 0.975 | 0.960 | 0.993 |

Table 4: Pearson correlation between productivity and evaluation measures.

Finally, another advantage of the fuzzy metric is the fact that it does not depend on tokenization. It is a well known-fact that depending on the tokenization applied to the MT output and the reference, differences in BLEU arise. This is illustrated in Table 5, which reports the BLEU scores obtained for the MT post-edited text as estimated by different tools: Asiya (Giménez and Màrquez, 2010), Asia Online's Language Studio[12], and the multibleu script included in the SMT system MOSES (Koehn et al., 2007). As can be observed, there are significant differences in BLEU scores for the same band for both translators.

| | **BLEU (Asiya)** | **BLEU (Asia Online)** | **BLEU (MOSES)** |
|---|---|---|---|
| *Trans. 1* | | | |
| **100%** | 91.96 | 91.94 | 91.96 |
| **95-99%** | 87.91 | 87.77 | 87.20 |
| **85-94%** | 80.19 | 80.12 | 80.20 |
| **75-84%** | 73.94 | 74.27 | 74.09 |
| **PE** | 69.57 | 68.93 | 69.37 |
| *Trans. 2* | | | |
| **100%** | 92.38 | 92.37 | 92.39 |
| **95-99%** | 89.35 | 89.22 | 89.19 |
| **85-94%** | 81.00 | 80.94 | 80.97 |
| **75-84%** | 71.98 | 72.55 | 72.12 |
| **PE** | 66.37 | 65.66 | 66.16 |

Table 5: BLEU results as computed by different evaluation tools.

## 5 Conclusion and Future work

In this paper, we have reported a pilot experiment based on a real-life translation project. The translation job was analyzed with the usual CAT tools in our company to ensure the project included samples of all TM match bands. All matches below 75% TM fuzzy leverage were then split into two parts: one was used for MTPE, and the other half was translated from scratch. The raw MT output was generated by a customized Systran RBMT system and integrated in the CAT environment used to run the experiment.

We have discovered that MT quality may also be assessed using a fuzzy score mirroring TM leverage (we used 3-gram Sørensen-Dice coefficient). It correlates with productivity as well as or even better than BLEU and TER, it is easier to estimate[13], and does not depend on tokenization. Moreover, this metric is more familiar to all parties in the translation industry, as they already work with fuzzy matches when processing translation jobs via CAT tools.

Another interesting finding is that MTPE might result in an increased productivity ratio if the translator already has MTPE experience and is familiarized with the client's texts. However, further research on this matter is needed to confirm the impact of each factor separately.

The results of this pilot study reveal that a "fuzzier" approach might be a valid MTPE evaluation measure. In future work we plan to repeat the experiment with more translators to see if the findings reported here replicate. We believe that the proposed fuzzy-match approach, if proven valid, would be more easily embraced in MTPE workflows than more traditional evaluation measures.

## Acknowledgments

The research reported in this paper is supported by the People Programme (Marie Curie Actions) of the European Union's Framework Programme (FP7/2007-2013) under REA grant agreement nº 317471.

## References

Wilker Aziz, Sheila C. M. de Sousa, and Lucia Specia. 2012. PET; a Tool for Post-Editing and Assessing Machine Translation. In *Eighth International Conference on Language Resources and Evaluation (LREC 12)*, pages 3982–3987, Istanbul, Turkey, May. ELRA.

Lee R. Dice. 1945. Measures of the Amount of

[12] `http://www.asiaonline.net/EN/Default.aspx`

[13] There are free open-source tools (e.g. Okapi Rainbow) which support industry-standard bilingual files (XLIFF and TMX) able to calculate fuzzy scores.

Ecologic Association Between Species. *Ecological Society of America*, 26(3):297–302, July.

Marcello Federico, Alessandro Cattelan, and Marco Trombetti. 2012. Measuring User Productivity in Machine Translation Enhanced Computer Assisted Translation. In *Proceedings of the Tenth Conference of the Association for Machine Translation in the Americas (AMTA)*, San Diego, CA, October. AMTA.

Jesús Giménez and Lluís Màrquez. 2010. Asiya: An Open Toolkit for Automatic Machine Translation (Meta-)Evaluation. *The Prague Bulletin of Mathematical Linguistics*, (94):77–86.

Ana Guerberof Arenas. 2009. Productivity and quality in the post-editing of outputs from translation memories and machine translation. *The International Journal of Localisation*, 7, Issue 1:11–21.

Philipp Koehn, Hieu Hoang, Alexandra Birch, Chris Callison-Burch, Marcello Federico, Nicola Bertoldi, Brooke Cowan, Wade Shen, Christine Moran, Richard Zens, Chris Dyer, Ondrej Bojar, Alexandra Constantin, and Evan Herbst. 2007. Moses: Open Source Toolkit for Statistical Machine Translation. In *Annual Meeting of the Association for Computational Linguistics (ACL), demonstration session*, Prague, Czech Republic, June. ACL.

Philipp Koehn. 2010. *Statistical Machine Translation*. Cambridge University Press.

Alon Lavie, 2010. *Evaluating the Output of Machine Translation Systems*. AMTA, Denver, Colorado, USA, October.

Vladimir I. Levenshtein. 1965. Binary codes capable of correcting deletions, insertionsm, and reversals. *Soviet Physics Doklady*, 10(8):707–710, February.

John Moran, Christian Saam, and Dave Lewis. 2014. Towards desktop-based CAT tool instrumentation. In *Proceedings of the Third Workshop on Post-Editing Technology and Practice*, pages 99–112, Vancouver, BC, October. AMTA.

Kishore Papineni, Salim Roukos, Todd Ward, and Wei-Jing Zhu. 2001. Bleu: a Method for Automatic Evaluation of Machine Translation. IBM Research Report RC22176 (W0109-022), IBM Research Division, Thomas J. Watson Research Center, P.O. Box 218, Yorktown Heights, NY 10598, September.

Matthew Snover, Bonnie Dorr, Richard Schwartz, Linnea Micciulla, and John Makhoul. 2006. A Study of Translation Edit Rate with Targeted Human Annotation. In *Proceedings of the 7th Conference of the Association for Machine Translation in the Americas*, pages 223–231, Cambridge, Massachusetts, USA, August.

Thorvald Sørensen. 1948. A method of establishing groups of equal amplitude in plant sociology based on similarity of species and its application to analyses of the vegetation on Danish commons. *Kongelige Danske Videnskabernes Selskab*, 5 (4):1–34.

# A Methodology for Bilingual Lexicon Extraction from Comparable Corpora

**Reinhard Rapp**
University of Mainz, FTSK
An der Hochschule 2
D-76726 Germersheim
reinhardrapp@gmx.de

## Abstract

Dictionary extraction using parallel corpora is well established. However, for many language pairs parallel corpora are a scarce resource which is why in the current work we discuss methods for dictionary extraction from comparable corpora. Hereby the aim is to push the boundaries of current approaches, which typically utilize correlations between co-occurrence patterns across languages, in several ways: 1) Eliminating the need for initial lexicons by using a bootstrapping approach which only requires a few seed translations. 2) Implementing a new approach which first establishes alignments between comparable documents across languages, and then computes cross-lingual alignments between words and multiword-units. 3) Improving the quality of computed word translations by applying an interlingua approach, which, by relying on several pivot languages, allows an effective multi-dimensional cross-check. 4) We investigate that, by looking at foreign citations, language translations can even be derived from a single monolingual text corpus.

## 1 Introduction

The aim of this paper is to suggest new methods for automatically extracting bilingual dictionaries, i.e. dictionaries listing all possible translations of words and multiword units, from comparable corpora. With comparable corpora we mean sets of text collections which cover roughly the same subject area in different languages or dialects, but which are not translations of each other. Their main advantages are that they don't have a translation bias (as there is no source language which could show through) and are available in by far larger quantities and for more domains than parallel corpora, i.e. collections of translated texts.

The systems to be developed are supposed to have virtually no prior knowledge on word translations. Instead, they induce this knowledge statistically using an extension of Harris' distributional hypothesis (Harris, 1954) to the multilingual case. The distributional hypothesis states that words occurring in similar contexts have related meanings. Its application led to excellent automatically created monolingual thesauri of related words. Our extension of Harris' distributional hypothesis to the multilingual case claims that the translations of words with related meanings will also have related meanings. From this it can be inferred that if two words co-occur more frequently than expected in a corpus of one language, then their translations into another language will also co-occur more frequently than expected in a comparable corpus of this other language. This is the primary statistical clue which is the basis for our work. Starting from this our aim is to develop a methodology which is capable of deriving good quality bilingual dictionaries in a language independent fashion, i.e. which can be applied to all language pairs where comparable corpora are available. In future work, to exemplify the results achieved with this method, we will generate large dictionaries comprising single words and multiword units for the following language pairs: English–German; English–French; English–Spanish; German–French; German–Spanish; French–Spanish, German–Dutch, and Spanish–Dutch.

Bilingual dictionaries are an indispensable resource for both human and machine translation. For



*Proceedings of the ACL 2015 Fourth Workshop on Hybrid Approaches to Translation (HyTra)*, pages 46–55,
Beijing, China, July 31, 2015. 

this reason, in the field of lexicography a lot of effort has been put into producing high quality dictionaries. For example, in rule-based machine translation producing the dictionaries is usually by far the most time consuming and expensive part of system development. But as the dictionaries are crucial in ensuring high coverage and high translation quality, a lot of effort has to be invested into them, and there are many examples where the manual creation of comprehensive dictionaries has been an ongoing process over several decades. Now that some high quality dictionaries exist, why do we suggest further research in this field? The reasons are manifold:

1) High quality dictionaries are only available for a few hundred common language pairs, usually involving some of the major European and Asian languages. But there exist about 7000 languages worldwide (Gordon & Grimes, 2005; Katzner, 2002), of which 600 have a written form. In the interest of speakers or learners of lesser used languages, at least for all possible pairs of written languages high quality dictionaries would be desirable, which means a total of 600 * (600 – 1) = 359,400 translation directions. But in practice this is impossible for reasons of time, effort, and cost. So the companies working in the field tend to concentrate on their major markets only.
2) The usage and meanings of words are adapted and modified in language of specialized domains and genres. To give an example, the word *memory* is used differently in the life sciences and in computer science. This means that in principle for each domain specific dictionaries would be desirable. Again, for a few common language pairs and commercially important subject areas such as medicine or engineering such dictionaries have been developed. But if we (conservatively) assumed only 20 subject areas, the total number of required dictionaries increases from 359,400 to 143,988,000.
3) Languages evolve over time. New topics and disciplines require the creation or borrowing (e.g. from English) of new terms (a good example is mobile computing), other terms become obsolete. This means that we cannot create our dictionaries once and forever, but need to constantly track these changes, for all language pairs, and for all subject areas.
4) Even if some companies such as specialized publishing houses (e.g. *Collins* and *Oxford University Press*), translation companies (e.g. *Systran* and *SDL*) or global players (e.g. *Google* and *Microsoft*) can afford to compile dictionaries for some markets, these dictionaries are proprietary and often not available for other companies, institutions, academia, and individuals. This is an obstacle for the advancement of the field.

Given this situation, it would be desirable to be able to generate dictionaries ad hoc as we need them from corpora of the text types we are interested in. So a lot of thought has been spent on how to produce bilingual dictionaries more efficiently than manually in the traditional lexicographic way. From these efforts, two major straits of research arose: The first is based on the exploitation of parallel corpora, i.e. collections of translated documents, as suggested by Brown et al. (1990 and 1993) in their seminal papers. They automatically extracted a bilingual dictionary from a large parallel corpus of English–French Canadian parliamentary proceedings, and then built a machine translation system around this. The development of such systems has not been without setbacks, but finally, after 15 years of research, it led to a revolution in machine translation technology and provided the basis for machine translation systems such as *Moses*, *Google Translate* and Microsoft's *Bing Translator* which are used by millions of people worldwide every day.

The second strait of research is based on comparable rather than parallel corpora. It was first suggested by Fung (1995) and Rapp (1995). The motivation was that parallel corpora are a scarce resource for most language pairs and subject areas, and that human performance in second language acquisition and in translation shows that there must be a way of crossing the language barrier that does not require the reception of large amounts of translated texts. We suggest here to replace parallel by comparable corpora. Comparable (written or spoken) corpora are far more abundant than parallel corpora, thus offering the chance to overcome the data acquisition bottleneck. This is particularly true as, given $n$ languages to be considered, $n$ comparable corpora will suffice. In contrast, with parallel corpora, unless translations of the same text are available in several languages, the number of required corpora $c$ increases quadratically with the number of languages as $c = (n^2 - n)/2$.

However, the problem with comparable corpora is that it is much harder to extract a bilingual dictionary from comparable corpora than from parallel corpora. As a consequence, despite intensive research carried out over two decades (to a good part taking place in international projects such as *AC-*

*CURAT*, *HyghTra*, *PRESEMT*, METIS, *Kelly*, and *TTC*) no commercial breakthrough has yet been possible.

However, we feel that in recent years some remarkable improvements were suggested (e.g. dictionary extraction from aligned comparable documents and dictionary verification using cross checks based on pivot languages). They cannot solve the problem when used in isolation, but when amended and combined they may well have the potential to lead to substantial improvements. In this paper we try to come up with a roadmap for this.

## 2 Methodology

Although, if at all, it is more likely that the mechanisms underlying human second language acquisition are based on the processing of comparable rather than parallel corpora, we do not attempt to simulate the complexities of human second language acquisition. Instead we argue that it is possible by purely technical means to automatically extract information on word- and multiword-translations from comparable corpora. The aim is to push the boundaries of current approaches, which often utilize similarities between co-occurrence patterns across languages, in several ways:

1. Eliminating the need for initial dictionaries.
2. Looking at aligned comparable documents rather than at comparable corpora.
3. Utilizing multiple pivot languages in order to improve dictionary quality.
4. Considering word senses rather than words in order to solve the ambiguity problem.
5. Investigate in how far foreign citations in monolingual corpora are useful for dictionary generation.
6. Generating dictionaries of multiword units.
7. Applying the approach to different text types.
8. Developing a standard test set for evaluation.

Let us now look point by point at the above list of research objectives with an emphasis on methodological and innovative aspects.

### 2.1 Eliminating the need for initial dictionaries

The standard approach for the generation of dictionaries using comparable corpora operates in three steps: 1) In the source language, find the words frequently co-occurring with a given word whose translation is to be determined. 2) Translate these frequently co-occurring words into the target language using an initial dictionary. 3) In the target language, find the word which most frequently co-occurs with these translations.

There are two major problems with this approach: Firstly, an already relatively comprehensive initial dictionary of typically more than 10,000 entries (Rapp, 1999) is required which will often be a problem for language pairs involving lesser used languages or when existing dictionaries are copyright protected or not available in machine readable form. Secondly, depending on the coverage of this dictionary, quite a few of the requested translations may not be known. For these reasons a method not requiring an initial dictionary would be desirable. Let us therefore outline our proposal for a novel bootstrapping approach which requires only a few seed translations. The underlying idea is based on multi-stimulus associations (Rapp, 1996; Rapp, 2008; Lafourcade & Zampa, 2009; Rapp & Zock, 2014). There is also related work in cognitive science. It often goes under the label of the *remote association test*, but essentially pursues the same ideas (Smith et al., 2013).

As experience tells, associations to several stimuli are non-random. For example, if we present the word pair *circus – laugh* to test persons and ask for their spontaneous associations, a typical answer will be *clown*. Likewise, if we present *King – daughter*, many will respond with *princess*. Like the associative responses to single words, the associative answers to pairs of stimuli can also be predicted with high precision by looking at the co-occurrences of words in text corpora. A nice feature about the word pair associations is that the number of possible word pairs increases with the square of the vocabulary size considered. For a vocabulary of *n* words, the number of possible pairwise combinations (and likewise the number of associations) is $n * (n - 1) / 2$. This means that for a vocabulary of 10 words we have 45, for a vocabulary of 100 words we have 4,950, and for a vocabulary of 1000 words we have 499,500 possible word pairs, and each of these pairs provides valuable information.[1]

[1] As will become later on, this is actually one of the rare cases where large numbers work in favour of us, thus making the method well suited for the suggested bootstrapping approach. This behavior is in contrast to most other applications in natural language processing. For example, in syntax parsing or in machine translation the number of possible parse trees or sentence translations tends to grow exponentially with the length of a sentence. But the higher the number of possibilities, the more difficult it gets to filter out the correct variant.

To exemplify the suggested approach, let us assume that our starting vocabulary consists of the four words *circus*, *laugh*, *King*, and *daughter*. We assume that their translations into the target language are known. If our target language is German, the translations are *Zirkus*, *lachen*, *König*, and *Tochter*. Separately for the source and the target language, based on corpus evidence we compute the multi-stimulus associations for all possible word pairs (compare Rapp, 2008):

*English:*
circus – laugh → clown
circus – King → lion
circus – daughter → artiste
laugh – King → jester
laugh – daughter → joke
King – daughter → princess

*German:*
Zirkus – lachen → Clown
Zirkus – König → Löwe
Zirkus – Tochter → Artistin
Lachen – König → Hofnarr
lachen – Tochter → Witz
König – Tochter → Prinzessin

Now our basic assumption is that the corresponding English and German multi-stimulus associations are translations of each other. This means that to our initial four seed translations we can now add a further six newly acquired translations, namely *clown → Clown, lion → Löwe, artiste → Artistin, jester → Hofnarr, joke → Witz, princess → Prinzessin.* Together with the four seed translations, this gives us a total of ten known translations. With these ten translations we can restart the process, this time with a much higher number of possible pairs (45 pairs of which 35 are new). Once this step is completed, ideally we would have 45 * (45 – 1) / 2 = 990 known translations. In continuation, with a few more iterations we cover a very large vocabulary.

Of course, for the purpose of demonstrating the approach we have idealized matters here. In reality, many word pairs will not have salient associations, so the associations which we compute can be somewhat arbitrary. This means that our underlying assumption, namely that word pair associations are equivalent across languages, may not hold for non-salient cases, and even when the associations are salient there can still be discrepancies caused by cultural, domain-dependent and other differences. For example, the word pair *pork – eat* might evoke the association *lunch* in one culture, but *forbidden* in another. But non-salient associations can be identified and eliminated by applying a significance test on the measured association strengths. And cultural differences are likely to be small in comparison to the commonalities of human life as expressed through language. Would this not be true, it should be almost impossible to translate between languages with different cultural backgrounds, but experience tells us that this is still possible (though more difficult).

It should also be noted that the suggested approach, like most statistical approaches used in NLP, should show a great deal of error tolerance. The iterative process should converge as long as the majority of computed translations is correct. Also, the associative methodology implies that incorrect translations will typically be caused by mixups between closely related words, which will limit the overall negative effect.

If required to ensure convergence, we can add further levels of sophistication such as the following: a) Compute salient associations not only for word pairs, but also for word triplets (e.g. *pork – eat – Muslim → forbidden*; *pork – eat – Christian → ok*). b) Use translation probabilities rather than binary yes/no decisions. c) Use pivot languages to verify the correctness of the computed translations (see section 2.4 below). d) Look at aligned comparable documents (see below).

### 2.2 Looking at aligned comparable documents rather than at comparable corpora

Here we investigate an alternative approach to the above. It also does not require a seed lexicon, but instead has higher demands concerning the comparable corpora to be used. For this approach the comparable corpora need to be alignable at the document level, i.e. it must be possible to identify correspondences between the documents in two comparable corpora of different languages. This is straightforward e.g. for Wikipedia articles where the so-called interlanguage links (created manually by the authors) connect articles across languages. But there are many more common text types which are easily alignable, among them newspaper corpora where the date of publication gives an important clue, or scientific papers whose topics tend to be so narrow that a few specific internationalisms or proper names can be sufficient to identify the correspondences.

Once the alignment at the document level has been conducted, the next step is to identify the most salient keywords in each of the documents. There are a number of well established ways of doing so, among them Paul Rayson's method of comparing the observed term frequencies in a document to the average frequencies in a reference corpus using the log-likelihood ratio, or – alternatively – the Likely-system as developed by Paukkeri & Honkela (2010). By applying these keyword extraction methods the aligned comparable documents are converted to aligned lists of keywords. Some important properties of these lists of aligned keywords are similar to those of aligned parallel sentences, which means that there is a chance to successfully apply the established statistical machinery developed for parallel sentences. We conducted a pilot study using a self-developed robust alternative to GIZA++, with promising results (Rapp, Sharoff & Babych, 2012). In principle, the method is applicable not only to the problem of identifying the translations of single words, but also of identifying the translations of multiword units, see section 2.6 below.

### 2.3 Utilizing multiple pivot languages in order to improve dictionary quality

We propose to systematically explore the possibility of utilizing the dictionaries' property of *transitivity*. What we mean by this is the following: If we have two dictionaries, one translating from language A to language B, the other from language B to language C, then we can also translate from A to C by using B as the pivot language (also referred to as bridge language, intermediate language, or interlingua). That is, the property of transitivity, although having some limitations due to the ambiguity problem, can be exploited for the automatic generation of a raw dictionary with mappings from A to C. On first glance, one might consider this unnecessary as our corpus-based approach allows us to generate such a dictionary with higher accuracy directly from the respective comparable corpora.

However, the above implies that we have now two ways of generating a dictionary for a particular language pair, which means that in principle we can validate one with the other. Furthermore, given several languages, there is not only one method to generate a transitivity-based dictionary for A to C, but there are several. This means that by increasing the number of languages we also increase the possibilities of mutual cross-validation. In this way a highly effective multi-dimensional cross-check can be realized.

Utilizing transitivity is a well established technique in manual dictionary lookup when people interested in uncommon language pairs (where no dictionary is available) use two dictionaries involving a common pivot language. Likewise, lexicographers often use this concept when manually creating dictionaries for new language pairs based on existing ones. However, this has not yet been explored at a large scale in a setting like ours. We propose to use many pivot languages in parallel, and to introduce a voting system where a potential translation of a source word is ranked according to the number of successful cross-validations.

### 2.4 Considering word senses rather than words in order to solve the ambiguity problem

As in natural language most words are ambiguous, and as the translation of a word tends to be ambiguous in a different way than the original source language word (especially if we look at unrelated languages belonging to different language families), our extension of Harris's distributional hypothesis which says that the translations of two related words should be related again (see Section 1) is only an approximation but not strictly applicable. But in principle it would be strictly applicable and therefore lead to better results if we conducted a word sense disambiguation on our comparable corpora beforehand. Hereby we assume that the sense inventories for the languages to be considered are similar in granularity and content.[2] We therefore propose to sense disambiguate the corpora, and to apply our method for identifying word translations on the senses. As a result, we will not only obtain a bilingual dictionary, but also an alignment of the two sense inventories.

As versions of *WordNet* are available for all five languages mentioned in Section 1 (English, French, German, Spanish, Dutch), we intend to use these WordNets as our sense inventories. Regarding some criticism that they are often too fine grained for practical applications (Navigli, 2009), we will consider attempts to automatically derive more coarse-grained sense inventories from them (Navigli et al., 2007). Given the resulting sense inventories, we will apply an open source word sense disambiguation algorithm such as Ted Pedersen's *SenseRelate* software (alternatives are *BabelNet*, *UKB* and other systems as e.g. used in the SemEval word sense disambiguation competitions).

Relying on the WordNet senses means that the methodology is not applicable to languages where a version of WordNet is not available. As this is a serious shortcoming, we have looked at methods for generating corpus-specific sense inventories in an unsupervised way (Pantel & Lin, 2002; Bordag,

[2] Similar sense inventories across languages can be expected under the assumption that the senses reflect observations in the real world.

2006; Rapp, 2003; SemEval 2007 and 2010 task "Word sense induction"). In an attempt to come up with an improved algorithm, we propose a novel bootstrapping approach which conducts word sense induction and word sense disambiguation in an integrated fashion. It starts by tagging each content word in a corpus with the strongest association that occurs nearby. For example, in the sentence "*He gets money from the bank*", the word *bank* would be tagged with *money* as this is the strongest association occurring in this neighborhood. Let us use the notation [bank < money] to indicate this. From the tagged corpus a standard distributional thesaurus is derived (Pantel & Lin, 2002). This thesaurus would, for example, show that [bank < money] is closely related to [bank < account], but not to [bank < river]. For this reason, all occurrences of [bank < money] and [bank < account] would be replaced by [bank < money, account], but [bank < river] would remain unchanged. Likewise for all other strongly related word/tag combinations. Subsequently, in a second iteration a new distributional thesaurus is computed, leading to further mergers of word/tag combinations. This iterative process is to be repeated until there are no more strong similarities between any entries of a newly created thesaurus. At this point the result is a fully sense tagged corpus where the granularity of the senses can be controlled as it depends on the similarity threshold used for merging thesaurus entries.

### 2.5 Investigating in how far foreign citations in monolingual corpora can be utilized for dictionary generation

Traditional foreign language teaching, where the teacher explains the foreign language using the native tongue of the students, has often been criticized. But there can be no doubt that it works at least to some extent. Apparently, the language mix used in such a teaching environment is non-random, which is why we start from the hypothesis that it should be possible to draw conclusions on word translations given a corpus of such classroom transcripts. We suggest that the translations of words can be discovered by looking at strong associations between the words of the teaching language and the words of the foreign language. In a 2nd-language teaching environment the words of the foreign language tend to be explained using corresponding words from the teaching language, i.e. these two types of words tend to co-occur more often than to be expected by chance.

However, as it is not easy to compile transcripts of such classroom communications in large enough quantities, we assume that the use of foreign language citations in large newspaper or web corpora follows similar principles (for a pilot study see Rapp & Zock, 2010b). The following two citations from the Brown Corpus (Francis & Kuçera, 1989) are meant to provide some evidence for this (underscores by us):

1. The tables include those for the classification angles , refractive indices , and melting points of the various types of crystals . Part 2 of Volume /1 , and Parts 2 and 3 of Volume /2 , contain the crystal descriptions . These are grouped into sections according to the crystal system , and within each section compounds are arranged in the same order as in Groth 's CHEMISCHE KRYSTALLOGRAPHIE . An alphabetical list of chemical and mineralogical names with reference numbers enables one to find a particular crystal description . References to the data sources are given in the crystal descriptions .

2. On the right window , at eye level , in smaller print but also in gold , was Gonzalez , Prop. , and under that , Se Habla Espanol . Mr. Phillips took a razor to Gonzalez , Prop. , but left the promise that Spanish would be understood because he thought it meant that Spanish clientele would be welcome .

In the first example, the German book title "Chemische Krystallographie"[3] (meaning *Chemical Crystallography*) is cited. In its context the word *chemical* occurs once and the word forms *crystal* and *crystals* occur five times. In the second example, the phrase "Se Habla Espanol" is cited (meaning: *Spanish spoken* or *We speak Spanish*), and in its context we find "Spanish would be understood" which comes close to a translation of this phrase. (And a few words further in the same sentence the word "Spanish" occurs again.)

Although foreign language citations are usually scarce in standard corpora, lexicon extraction from monolingual corpora should still be feasible for heavily cited languages such as English. For other languages lexicon construction should be possible via pivot languages, see Section 2.3 above. The problem that the same word form can occur in several languages but with different meanings (called "homograph trap" in Rapp & Zock, 2010b) can be approached by looking at several source languages at the same time and by eliminating interpretations which are not consistent with several of the languages. We intend to apply this method to all language pairs, and use it in a supplementary fashion to enhance the other approaches. This looks prom-

[3] Note that *Krystallographie* is an old spelling. The modern spelling is *Kristallographie*.

ising as the method provides independent statistical clues from a different type of source.

### 2.6 Generating dictionaries of multiword units

Due to their sheer numbers, the treatment of multiword units is a weakness of traditional lexicography. Whereas a reasonable coverage of single words may require in the order of 100,000 dictionary entries, the creation of multiword units is highly productive so that their number can be orders of magnitude higher, making it infeasible to achieve good coverage using manual methods. In contrast, most automatic methods for dictionary extraction, including the ones described above, can be applied to multiword units in a straightforward way. The only prerequisite is that the multiword units need to be known beforehand, that is, in a pre-processing step they must be identified and tagged as such in the corpora. There exist numerous methods for this, most of them relying on measures of mutual information between neighbouring words (e.g. Smadja, 1993; Paukkeri & Honkela, 2010). Our intention is to adopt the language independent "Likely" system for this purpose (Paukkeri & Honkela, 2010). Using the methods described in Sections 2.1 to 2.5, we will generate dictionaries of multiword units for all language pairs considered, i.e. involving English, French, German, Spanish, and Dutch, and then evaluate the dictionaries as outlined in section 2.8.

Our expectation is that the problem of word ambiguity will be less severe with multiword units than it is with single words. There are two reasons for this, which are probably two sides of the same medal: One is that rare words tend to be less ambiguous than frequent words, as apparently in human language acquisition a minimum number of observations is required to learn a reading, and the chances to reach this minimum number are lower for rare words. As multiword units are less frequent than their rarest constituents, on average their frequencies are lower than the frequencies of single words. Therefore it can be expected that they must be less ambiguous on average. The other explanation is that in multiword units the constituents tend to disambiguate each other, so fewer readings remain.

### 2.7 Applying the approach to different text types

By their nature, the dictionaries generated using the above algorithms will always reflect the contents of the underlying corpora, i.e. their genre and topic. This means that if the corpora consist of newspaper articles on politics, the generated dictionaries will reflect this use of language, and likewise with other genres and topics. It is of interest to investigate these effects. However, as for a reasonable coverage and quality of the extracted dictionaries we need large corpora (e.g. larger than 50 million words) for all five languages, we feel that for a first study it is only realistic to make just a few rough distinctions in a somewhat opportunistic way: a) newspaper articles; b) parliamentary proceedings; c) encyclopaedic articles; d) general web documents. The resulting dictionaries will be compared qualitatively and quantitatively. However, in the longer term it will of course be of interest to aim for more fine-grained distinctions of genre and topic.

### 2.8 Developing a standard test set for evaluation

As previous evaluations of the dictionary extraction task were usually conducted with ad hoc test sets and thus were not comparable, Laws et al. (2010) noted an urgent need for standard test sets. In response to this, we intend to work out and publish a gold standard which covers all of our eight language pairs and will ensure that words of a wide range of frequencies are appropriately represented. All results on single words are to be evaluated using this test set.

Little work has been done so far on multiword dictionary extraction using comparable corpora (an exception is Rapp & Sharoff, 2010), and no widely accepted gold standard exists. A problem is that there are many ways how to define multiword units. To explore these and to provide for different needs, we aim for five types of test sets of at least 5000 multiword units and their translations. The test sets are to be generated semi-automatically in the following ways:

a) Multiword units connected by Wikipedia interlanguage links.
b) Multiword units extracted from a parallel corpus which was word-aligned using GIZA++.
c) Multiword units extracted from phrase tables as generated using the Moses toolkit.
d) Multiword units extracted with a co-occurrence based system such as *Likely* (Paukkeri & Honkela, 2010) and redundantly translated with several translation systems, using voting to select translations.
e) Multiword named entities taken from *JRC-Names* (as provided by the European Commission's Joint Research Centre).

The results on the multiword dictionary extraction task are to be evaluated using each of these gold standards.

## 3 Discussion

In this section we discuss the relationship of the suggested work to the state of the art of research in the field. Hereby we concentrate on how the previous literature relates to the eight subtopics listed above. A more comprehensive survey of the field of bilingual dictionary extraction from comparable corpora can be found in Sharoff et al. (2013).

1) *Eliminating the need for initial dictionaries:* This problem has been approached e.g. by Rapp (1995), Diab & Finch (2000), Haghighi et al. (2008), and Vulic & Moens (2012). None of the suggested solutions seems to work well enough for most practical purposes. Through its multilevel approach, the above methodology aims to achieve this.
2) *Looking at aligned comparable documents rather than at comparable corpora:* Previous publications concerning this are Schafer & Yarowsky (2002), Hassan & Mihalcea (2009), Prochasson & Fung (2011) and Rapp et al. (2012). In our view, the full potential has not yet been unveiled.
3) *Utilizing multiple pivot languages in order to improve dictionary quality:* The (to our knowledge) only previous study in such a context was conducted by ourselves (Rapp & Zock, 2010a), and uses only a single pivot language. In contrast, here we suggest to take advantage of multiple pivot languages.[4]
4) *Considering word senses rather than words in order to solve the ambiguity problem:* Gaussier et al. (2004) use a geometric view to decompose the word vectors according to their senses. In contrast, we will use explicit word sense disambiguation based on the WordNet sense inventory. Annotations consistent with human intuitions are easier to verify and thus the system can be better optimized.
5) *Investigating in how far foreign citations in monolingual corpora can be used for dictionary generation:* To our knowledge, apart from our own (see Rapp & Zock, 2010b) there is no other previous work on this.
6) *Generating dictionaries of multiword units:* Robitaille et al. (2006) and the TTC project (http://www.ttc-project.eu/) dealt with this in a comparable corpora setting but did not make their results available. In contrast, the intention here is to publish the full dictionaries.
7) *Applying the approach to different text types:* Although different researchers used a multitude of comparable corpora, to our knowledge there exists no systematic comparative study concerning different text types in the field of bilingual dictionary extraction.
8) *Developing a standard test set for evaluation:* Laws et al. (2010) pointed out the need for a common test set and provided one for the language pair English – German. Otherwise in most cases ad hoc test sets were used, and to our knowledge no readily available test set exists for multiword units.

## 4 Conclusions

A core problem in NLP is the problem of ambiguity in a multilingual setting. Entities in natural language tend to be ambiguous but can be interpreted as mixtures of some underlying unambiguous entities (e.g. a word's senses). The problem in simulating, understanding, and translating natural language is that we can only observe and study the complicated behavior of the ambiguous entities, whereas the presumably simpler behavior of the underlying unambiguous entities remains hidden. The proposed work shows a way how to deal with this problem. This is relevant to most other fields in natural language processing where the ambiguity problem is also of central importance, such as MT, question answering, text summarization, thesaurus construction, information retrieval, information extraction, text classification, text data mining, speech recognition, and the semantic web.

The suggested work investigates new methods for the automatic construction of bilingual dictionaries, which are a fundamental resource in human translation, second language acquisition, and machine translation. If approached in the traditional lexicographic way, the creation of such resources has often taken years of manual work involving numerous subjective and potentially controversial decisions. In the suggested framework, these human intuitions are replaced by automatic processes which are based on corpus evidence. The developed systems will be largely language independent and will be applied to eight project language pairs involving the five European languages mentioned in Section 1. The suggested approach is of interest

[4] We use here the term *pivot language* as the potentially alternative term *bridge language* is used by Schafer &Yarowsky (2002) in a different sense, relating to orthographic similarities.

as the recent advances in the field concerning e.g. bootstrapping algorithms, alignment of comparable documents, and word sense disambiguation were conducted in isolated studies but need to be amended, combined, and integrated into a single system.

For human translation, by preparing the resulting dictionaries in XML they can be made compatible for use with standard Translation Memory systems. This way they are available for professional translation (especially in technical translation, technical writing, and interpreting) where there is a high demand in specialized dictionaries, thus supporting globalization and internationalization.

The work is also of interest from a cognitive perspective, as a bilingual dictionary can be seen as a collection of human intuitions across languages. The question is if these intuitions do find their counterpart in corpus evidence. Should this be the case, this would support the view that human language acquisition can be explained by unsupervised learning on the basis of perceived spoken and written language. If not, other sources of information available for language learning would have to be identified, which may, for example, include an equivalent of Chomsky's language acquisition device.

## Acknowledgments

This research was supported by a Marie Curie Career Integration Grant within the 7th European Community Framework Programme. I would like to thank Silvia Hansen-Schirra for her support of this work and valuable comments.

## References

Brown, P.F., Cocke, J., Della Pietra, S.A., Della Pietra, V.J., Jelinek, F., Lafferty, J.D., Mercer, R.L., Roossin, P.S. (1990). A statistical approach to machine translation. *Computational Linguistics* 16(2), 79–85.

Brown, P., Pietra, S.D., Pietra, V.D., Mercer, R. (1993): The mathematics of statistical machine translation: parameter estimation. *Computational Linguistics* 19(2), 263–312.

Bordag, S. (2006). Word sense induction: triplet-based clustering and automatic evaluation. *Proceedings of EACL 2006*, Trento, Italy. 137–144.

Diab, M., Finch, S. (2000): A statistical wordlevel translation model for comparable corpora. *Proceedings of the Conference on Content-Based Multimedia Information Access* (RIAO).

Francis, W. Nelson; Kuçera, Henry (1989). *Manual of Information to Accompany a Standard Corpus of Present-Day Edited American English, for Use with Digital Computers.* Providence, R.I.: Brown University, Department of Linguistics.

Fung, P. (1995). Compiling bilingual lexicon entries from a non-parallel English-Chinese corpus. *Proceedings of the Third Annual Workshop on Very Large Corpora*, Boston, Massachusetts. 173–183.

Gaussier, E., Renders, J.M., Matveeva, I., Goutte, C., Djean, H. (2004). A geometric view on bilingual lexicon extraction from comparable corpora. *Proceedings of the 42nd ACL*, Barcelona, Spain, 526–533.

Gordon, R. G.; Grimes, B. F. (eds.) (2005). *Ethnologue: Languages of the World.* SIL International, Dallas, TX, USA, 15th edition.

Haghighi, A., Liang, P., Berg-Kirkpatrick, T., Klein, D. (2008): Learning bilingual lexicons from monolingual corpora. *Proceedings of ACL-HLT 2008*, Columbus, Ohio. 771–779.

Harris, Z.S. (1954). Distributional structure. *Word*, 10(23), 146–162.

Hassan, S., Mihalcea, R. (2009): Cross-lingual semantic relatedness using encyclopedic knowledge. *Proceedings of EMNLP.*

Katzner, K. (2002). *The Languages of the World.* Routledge, London/New York, 3rd edition.

Lafourcade, M.; Zampa, V. (2009). JeuxDeMots and PtiClic: games for vocabulary assessment and lexical acquisition. *Proceedings of Computer Games, Multimedia & Allied Technology 09* (CGAT'09). Singapore.

Laws, F.; Michelbacher, L.; Dorow, B.; Scheible, C.; Heid, U.; Schütze, H. (2010). A linguistically grounded graph model for bilingual lexicon extraction. *Proceedings of COLING 2010*, Beijing, China.

Navigli, R. (2009). Word Sense Disambiguation: A Survey. *ACM Computing Surveys*, Vol. 41, No. 2, Article 10.

Navigli, R.; Litkowski, K.; Hargraves, O. (2007). SemEval-2007 task 07: Coarse-grained English all-words task. *Proceedings of the Semeval-2007 Workshop at ACL 2007*, Prague, Czech Republic.

Pantel, P.; Lin, D. (2002). Discovering word senses from text. *Proceedings of ACM SIGKDD*, Edmonton, 613–619.

Paukkeri, M.-S.; Honkela, T. (2010). Likey: unsupervised language-independent keyphrase extraction. *Proceedings of the 5th International Workshop on Semantic Evaluation (SemEval) at ACL 2012*, 162–165.

Prochasson, E., Fung, P. (2011). Rare word translation extraction from aligned comparable documents. *Proceedings of ACL-HLT*, Portland.

Rapp, R. (1995). Identifying word translations in non-parallel texts. *Proceedings of the 33rd ACL*, Cambridge, MA, 320–322.

Rapp, R. (1996). *Die Berechnung von Assoziationen*. Hildesheim: Olms.

Rapp, R. (1999): Automatic identification of word translations from unrelated English and German corpora. *Proceedings of the 37th ACL*, Maryland, 395–398.

Rapp, R. (2003). Word sense discovery based on sense descriptor dissimilarity. *Proceedings of the Ninth Machine Translation Summit*, 315–322.

Rapp, R. (2008). The computation of associative responses to multiword stimuli. *Proceedings of the Workshop on Cognitive Aspects of the Lexicon* (COGALEX) at Coling 2008, Manchester. 102–109.

Rapp, R.; Sharoff, S. (2014). Extracting multiword translations from aligned comparable documents. *Proceedings of the 3rd Workshop on Hybrid Approaches to Translation (HyTra)*. Gothenburg, Sweden.

Rapp, R., Sharoff, S., Babych, B. (2012). Identifying word translations from comparable documents without a seed lexicon. *Proceedings of the 8th Language Resources and Evaluation Conference, LREC 2012*, Istanbul, Turkey.

Rapp, R., Zock, M. (2010a). Automatic dictionary expansion using non-parallel corpora. In: Fink, A., Lausen, B., Ultsch, W.S.A. (eds.): *Advances in Data Analysis, Data Handling and Business Intelligence. Proceedings of the 32nd Annual Meeting of the GfKl*, 2008. Springer, Heidelberg.

Rapp, R., Zock, M. (2010b): The noisier the better: Identifying multilingual word translations using a single monolingual corpus. *Proceedings of the 4th International Workshop on Cross Lingual Information Access*, COLING 2010, Beijing, 16–25.

Rapp, R.; Zock, M. (2014). The CogALex-IV Shared Task on the Lexical Access Problem. *Proceedings of the 4th Workshop on Cognitive Aspects of the Lexicon (CogALex)*, COLING 2014, Dublin, Ireland, 1–14.

Robitaille, X., Sasaki, Y., Tonoike, M., Sato, S., Utsuro, T. (2006). Compiling French-Japanese terminologies from the web. *Proceedings of the 11th Conference of EACL*, Trento, Italy, 225–232.

Schafer, C., Yarowsky, D (2002).: Inducing translation lexicons via diverse similarity measures and bridge languages. *Proceedings of CoNLL.*

Sharoff, S.; Rapp, R.; Zweigenbaum, P. (2013). Overviewing important aspects of the last twenty years of research in comparable corpora. In: S. Sharoff, R. Rapp, P. Zweigenbaum, P. Fung (eds.): *Building and Using Comparable Corpora*. Heidelberg: Springer, 1–18.

Smadja, F. (1993). Retrieving collocations from text: Xtract. *Computational Linguistics* 19 (1), 143–177.

Smith, Kevin A.; Huber, David E.; Vul, Edward (2013). Multiply-constrained semantic search in the Remote Associates Test. *Cognition* 128, 64–75.

Vulic, Ivan; Moens, Marie-Francine (2012). Detecting highly confident word translations from comparable corpora without any prior knowledge. *Proceedings of the 13th Conference of the European Chapter of the Association for Computational Linguistics*, Avignon, France, 449–459.

# Ongoing Study for Enhancing Chinese-Spanish Translation with Morphology Strategies

**Marta R. Costa-jussà**[1]
Centro de Investigación en Computación, Instituto Politécnico Nacional, Mexico
[1]marta@nlp.cic.ipn.mx

**Abstract**

Chinese and Spanish have different morphology structures, which poses a big challenge for translating between this pair of languages. In this paper, we analyze several strategies to better generalize from the Chinese non-morphology-based language to the Spanish rich morphology-based language. Strategies use a first-step of Spanish morphology-based simplifications and a second-step of fullform generation. The latter can be done using a translation system or classification methods. Finally, both steps are combined either by concatenation in cascade or integration using a factored-based style. Ongoing experiments (based on the United Nations corpus) and their results are described.

## 1 Introduction

The structure of Chinese and Spanish differs at most linguistic levels, e.g. morphology, syntax and semantics. In this paper, we are focusing on reducing the gap between both languages at the level of morphology. On the one hand, Chinese is an isolating language, which means having a low morpheme per word ratio. On the other hand, Spanish is a fusional language, which means having a tendency to overlay many morphemes. The challenge when translating between Chinese and Spanish is bigger in the direction from Chinese to Spanish, given that the same Chinese word can generate multiple Spanish words. For example, the Chinese word *fàn* (in transcribed Pinyin) can be translated by *comer, como, comí, comeré*[1] which correspond to several tense flexions of the same verb and also by *comes, comiste, comerás*[2], all of which also correspond to several person flexions of the same verb. This poses a challenge in Statistical Machine Translation (SMT) because translations are learnt by co-ocurrence of words in both languages. When a word has multiple translations, it generates sparsity in the translation model.

In this study, we experiment with different strategies to add morphology knowledge in a standard phrase-based SMT system (Koehn et al., 2003) for the Chinese-to-Spanish translation direction. However, the presented techniques could be used for other pairs involving isolating and fusional languages. The rest of the paper is organized as follows. Section 2 reports a brief overview of the related work both in using morphology knowledge in SMT and in translating from Chinese-to-Spanish. Section 3 explains the theoretical framework of phrase-based SMT at a high level and the details of each strategy to introduce morphology in the mentioned system. Section 4 describes the experiments and first results obtained for each theoretical strategy presented. Finally, Section 5 concludes this ongoing research and outlines the future research directions.

## 2 Related Work

There are numerous studies which deal with morphology in the field of SMT. Without aiming at completeness, we cite works that:

- Preprocess the data to make the structure of both languages more similar by means of enriching (Avramidis and Koehn, 2008; Ueffing and Ney, 2003) or segmentation techniques in agglutinative (S.Virpioja et al., 2007) or fusional languages (Costa-jussà, 2015a)
- Modify models (Koehn and Hoang, 2007)
- Post-process the data (Toutanova et al., 2008; Bojar and Tamchyna, 2011; Formiga et al., 2013).

[1] *to eat, I eat, I ate, I will eat*
[2] *you eat, you ate, you will eat*



*Proceedings of the ACL 2015 Fourth Workshop on Hybrid Approaches to Translation (HyTra)*, pages 56–60,
Beijing, China, July 31, 2015. 

The research work in this area is being very active, e.g. PhD proposals using strategies based on deep learning (Gutierrez-Vasques, 2015).

Previous works on the Chinese-Spanish language pair focus on compiling corpus and using pivot stategies (Costa-jussà et al., 2012) and on building a Rule-Based Machine Translation (RBMT) system (Costa-jussà and Centelles, In Press 2015). A high-level description of the state-of-the-art of the translation on this language pair is detailed in (Costa-jussà, 2015b).

Our work mixes several strategies but basically it goes in the direction of (Formiga et al., 2013) that focuses on solving the challenge of morphology as a post-processing classification problem. The idea is to translate from Chinese to a morphology-based simplified Spanish and, then, re-generate the morphology by means of classification algorithms. The competitive advantage from this strategy is the rise of algorithms based on deep learning techniques that can achieve high success rates, e.g. (Collobert et al., 2011).

## 3 Theoretical Framework

The phrase-based SMT system (Koehn et al., 2003) is trained on a parallel corpus at the level of sentences. It learns co-ocurrences and each token in the training set is considered as a different one no matter if it is morphologically related. Therefore, in the extreme case where the word *canto*[3] is in the training set and the inflection of the same verb *canté*[4] is not, the latter is going to be considered an out-of-vocabulary word.

**Strategy 1.** One well-known strategy to face this challenge is to add a part-of-speech (POS) language model which evaluates the probability of the POS-sequences instead of the word sequences.

**Strategy 2.** This second strategy consists on doing a cascade of systems: first, translate from source to morphology-based simplified target; second, translate from this simplified target to fullform target as shown in Figure 3.

One straightforward simplification in morphology can be adopting lemmas as shown in Table 1.

**Strategy 3.** This third strategy is based on factored-based translation (Koehn and Hoang, 2007), which uses linguistic information of words,

[3] *I sing*
[4] *I sang*

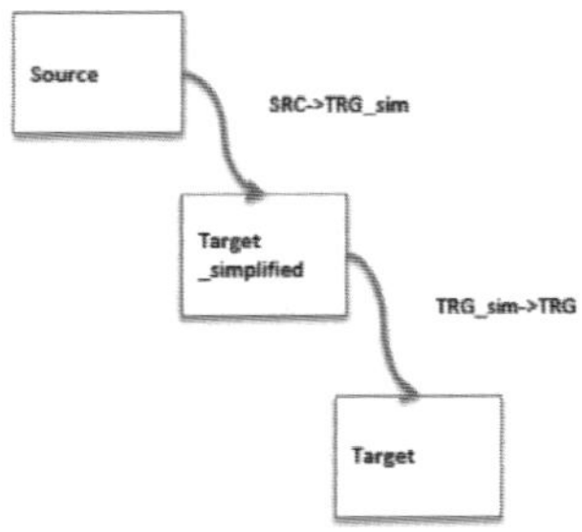


Figure 1: Illustration of the cascade strategy.

e.g. lemmas and POS. The idea is that the translation model based on words is used if the translation of the word is available, and if not, lemmas and POS are used in combination with a model to generate the final word. Figure 3 shows a typical representation of this factored strategy.

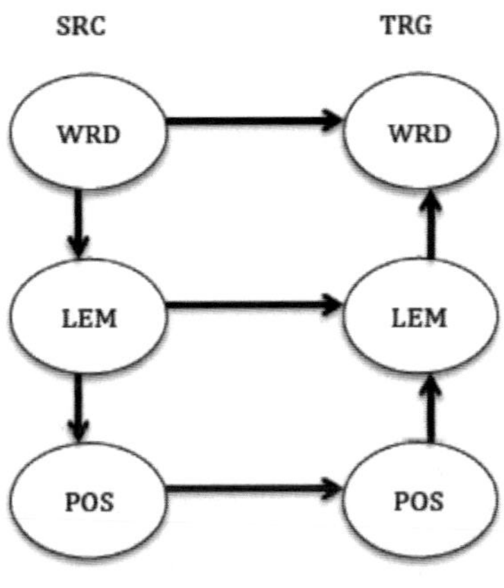


Figure 2: Illustration of the factored strategy.

**Strategy 4.** This fourth strategy is based on previous work like (Formiga et al., 2013), where the idea is to do a first translation from source to a morphology-based simplified target and then, use a classifier to go from this simplified target to the fullform target. See the schema of this classification-based strategy in 3.

The main challenges in the last strategy are:

1. Explore different simplifications of the target language in order to use the one with a higher trade-off between the highest oracle and the lowest classification complexity.

2. Explore several classification algorithms.

| | |
|---|---|
| $Es_{lemmas}$ | decidir examinar el cuestión en el período de sesión el tema titular " cuestión relativo a el derecho humano " |
| $Es^{N}_{lemmas}$ | Decide examinar la cuestión en el período de sesión el tema titulado " cuestión relativas a los derecho humanos " . |
| $Es^{V}_{lemmas}$ | decidir examinar la cuestión en el período de sesiones el tema titulado " Cuestiones relativas a los derechos humanos " . |
| $Es^{D}_{lemmas}$ | Decide examinar el cuestión en el período de sesiones el tema titulado " Cuestiones relativas a el derechos humanos " . |
| $Es^{P}_{lemmas}$ | Decide examinar la cuestión en el período de sesiones el tema titulado " Cuestiones relativas a los derechos humanos " . |
| $Es^{A}_{lemmas}$ | Decide examinar la cuestión en el período de sesiones el tema titular " Cuestiones relativo a los derechos humano " . |
| $Es_{tags}$ | VMIP3S0 VMN0000 DA0MS0 NCFS000 SPS00 DA0MS0 NCMS000 SPS00 NCFP000 DA0MS0 NCMS000 AQ0MS0 Fp NCFP000 AQ0FP0 SPS00 DA0MS0 NCMP000 AQ0MP0 Fp Fp |
| $Es_{num}$ | decidir[VMIP3**N**0] examinar[VMN0000] el[DA0M**N**0] cuestión[NCF**N**000] en[SPS00] el[DA0M**N**0] período[NCM**N**000] de[SPS00] sesión[NCF**N**000] el[DA0M**N**0] tema[NCM**N**000] titular[AQ0M**N**0] "[Fp] cuestión[NCF**N**000] relativo[AQ0F**N**0] a[SPS00] el[DA0M**N**0] derecho[NCM**N**000] humano[AQ0M**N**0] "[Fp] .[Fp] |
| $Es_{gen}$ | decidir[VMIP3S0] examinar[VMN0000] el[DA0**G**S0] cuestión[NC**G**S000] en[SPS00] el[DA0**G**S0] período[NC**G**S000] de[SPS00] sesión[NC**G**S000] el[DA0**G**S0] tema[NC**G**S000] titular[AQ0**G**S0] "[Fp] cuestión[NC**G**S000] relativo[AQ0**G**S0] a[SPS00] el[DA0**G**S0] derecho[NC**G**S000] humano[AQ0**G**S0] "[Fp] .[Fp] |
| $Es_{numgen}$ | decidir[VMIP3**N**0] examinar[VMN0000] el[DA0**GN**0] cuestión[NC**GN**000] en[SPS00] el[DA0**GN**0] período[NC**GN**000] de[SPS00] sesión[NC**GN**000] el[DA0**GN**0] tema[NC**GN**000] titular[AQ0**GN**0] "[Fp] cuestión[NC**GN**000] relativo[AQ0**GN**00] a[SPS00] el[DA0**GN**0] derecho[NC**GN**000] humano[AQ0**GN**0] "[Fp] .[Fp] |
| Es | Decide examinar la cuestión en el período de sesiones el tema titulado " Cuestiones relativas a los derechos humanos " . |

Table 1: Example of Spanish simplification into lemmas and different variations

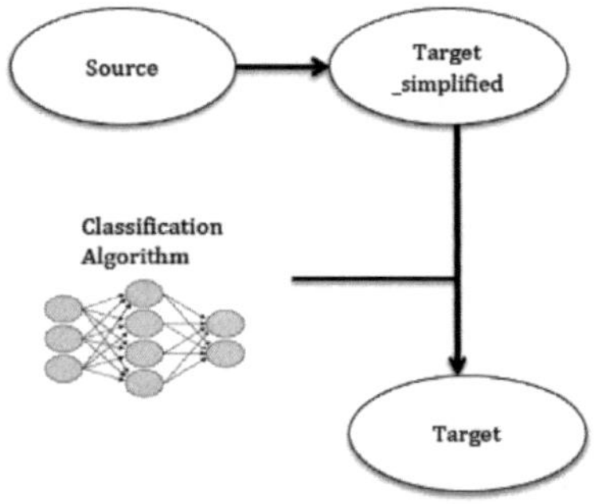


Figure 3: Illustration of the classification-based strategy.

In this paper, we study the first challenge of exploring different simplifications. However, we do not face the classification challenge, which is left to further work. It would be interesting to use deep learning knowledge which is leading to large improvements in natural language processing (Collobert et al., 2011).

## 4 Ongoing Experiments

In this section we show experiments and results with the four strategies proposed in the previous section.

As discussed in the literature, there are not many parallel corpora available for Chinese-Spanish (Costa-jussà et al., 2012). In this work, we use the data set from the United Nations (Rafalovitch and Dale, 2009). The training corpus contains about 60,000 sentences (and around 2 million words) and the development and test corpus contain 1,000 sentences each one. The baseline system is standard phrase-based SMT trained with Moses (Koehn et al., 2007), with the default parameters.

Table 2 shows results for the strategies 1, 2 and 3 in terms of BLEU (Papineni et al., 2002). From the BLEU scores, we see that strategy 1 gives slight improvements, but strategies 2 and 3 do not.

| Strategy | System | BLEU |
|---|---|---|
| | Baseline | 32.29 |
| 1 | $+LM_{pos}$ | 32.54 |
| 2 | Cascade | 31.80 |
| | $Zh2Es_{lemmas}$ | 36.40 |
| | $Es_{lemmas}2Es$ | 71.79 |
| 3 | +Generation | 32.11 |

Table 2: BLEU scores for Zh2Es translation task and different morphology strategies.

Table 3 shows several oracles for strategy 4 with different morphology-based simplifications of Spanish. Best oracles are for lemmas. Then, we explore other simplifications, including lemmatizing only: nouns (N), verbs (V), determiners (D), posesives (P) or adjectives (A). Non of these alternatives approach the best oracle from lemmatizing all words.

However, the interesting results are obtained when simplifying by number (*num*) and/or gender (*gen*). When simplifying number or gender, note that we use the information of lemmas and tags. When generalizing number, note that instead of using the information of singular (*S*) or plural (*P*) in the POS tag with the respective *S* or *P*, we use the generic *N*. Therefore, we generalize the information of number. Similarly when generalizing gender or both (*numgen*).

Oracles get closer to the lemmas simplification when only simplifying both number and gender in Spanish. This finding is relevant in the sense that it simplifies the classification task in the further work that we are considering.

| System | Oracles |
|---|---|
| Baseline | 32.29 |
| Zh2Es$_{lemmas}$ | 36.40 |
| Zh2Es$^{N}_{lemmas}$ | 32.44 |
| Zh2Es$^{V}_{lemmas}$ | 33.07 |
| Zh2Es$^{D}_{lemmas}$ | 33.53 |
| Zh2Es$^{P}_{lemmas}$ | 32.22 |
| Zh2Es$^{A}_{lemmas}$ | 24.50 |
| Zh2Es$_{num}$ | 34.05 |
| Zh2Es$_{gen}$ | 33.36 |
| Zh2Es$_{numgen}$ | **35.80** |

Table 3: Oracles for different generalizations. In bold, the most interesting finding.

Table 1 shows examples of all simplifications presented in previous Table 3. Note that simplifications in number and gender use lemmas plus POS tags to omit just the corresponding information that will need to be recovered in the classification stage.

## 5 Conclusions and Further Work

This paper presents an ongoing work on enhacing a standard phrase-based SMT system by dealing with morphology. We have reported several strategies including adding POS language modeling, experimenting with cascade systems and factored-based translation models. Only the first one reported improvements over the baseline. An additional strategy consists of studying different Spanish simplifications and then, generating the full-form with classification techniques. Experiments show that simplification only in gender and number almost achieves improvements as good as the simplification on lemmas. This is an interesting result that reduces the level of complexity for the classification task. As further work, we will use classification techniques based on deep learning.

## Acknowledgements

This work has been supported in part by Spanish Ministerio de Economía y Competitividad, contract TEC2012-38939-C03-02 as well as from the European Regional Development Fund (ERDF/FEDER) and the Seventh Framework Program of the European Commission through the International Outgoing Fellowship Marie Curie Action (IMTraP-2011-29951).

## References

E. Avramidis and P. Koehn. 2008. Enriching morphologically poor languages for statistical machine translation. In *Proc. of the conference of the Association for Computational Linguistics and Human Language Technology (ACL-HLT)*, pages 763–770.

O. Bojar and A. Tamchyna. 2011. Forms wanted: Training smt on monolingual data. In *Workshop of Machine Translation and Morphologically-Rich Languages*.

R. Collobert, J. Weston, L. Bottou, M. Karlen, K. Kavukcuoglu, and P. Kuksa. 2011. Natural language processing (almost) from scratch. *Journal of Machine Learning Research*, 12:2493–2537, November.

M. R. Costa-jussà and J. Centelles. In Press, 2015. Description of the chinese-to-spanish rule-based machine translation system developed with a hybrid combination of human annotation and statistical techniques. *ACM Transactions on Asian and Low-Resource Language Information Processing*.

M. R. Costa-jussà, C. A. Henríquez Q, and R. E. Banchs. 2012. Evaluating indirect strategies for chinese-spanish statistical machine translation. *Journal of Artificial Intelligence Research*, 45(1):761–780, September.

M. R. Costa-jussà. 2015a. Segmentation strategies to face morphology challenges in brazilian-portuguese/english statistical machine translation and its integration in cross-language information retrieval. *Computación y Sistemas*, In Press.

M. R. Costa-jussà. 2015b. Traducción automática entre chino y español: dónde estamos? *Komputer Sapiens*, 1.

L. Formiga, M. R. Costa-jussà, J. B. Mariño, J. A. R. Fonollosa, A. Barrón-Cedeño, and L. Márquez. 2013. The TALP-UPC phrase-based translation systems for WMT13: System combination with morphology generation, domain adaptation and corpus filtering. In *Proceedings of the Eighth Workshop on Statistical Machine Translation*, pages 134–140, Sofia, Bulgaria, August.

X. Gutierrez-Vasques. 2015. Bilingual lexicon extraction for a distant language pair using a small parallel corpus. In *Proc. of the NAACL Student Research Workshop*.

P. Koehn and H. Hoang. 2007. Factored translation models. In *Proceedings of the 2007 Joint*

*Conference on Empirical Methods in Natural Language Processing and Computational Natural Language Learning (EMNLP-CoNLL)*, pages 868–876, Prague, Czech Republic, June. Association for Computational Linguistics.

P. Koehn, F.J. Och, and D. Marcu. 2003. Statistical Phrase-Based Translation. In *Proc. of the 41th Annual Meeting of the Association for Computational Linguistics.*

P. Koehn, H. Hoang, A. Birch, C. Callison-Burch, M. Federico, N. Bertoldi, B. Cowan, W. Shen, C. Moran, R. Zens, C. Dyer, O. Bojar, A. Constantin, and E. Herbst. 2007. Moses: Open Source Toolkit for Statistical Machine Translation. In *Proceedings of the 45th Annual Meeting of the ACL on Interactive Poster and Demonstration Sessions*, ACL '07, pages 177–180, Stroudsburg, PA, USA. Association for Computational Linguistics.

K Papineni, S. Roukos, T. Ward, and W.-J. Zhu. 2002. BLEU: A method for automatic evaluation of machine translation. In *Proceedings of the 40th Annual Meeting on Association for Computational Linguistics*, ACL '02, pages 311–318, Stroudsburg, PA, USA. Association for Computational Linguistics.

A. Rafalovitch and R. Dale. 2009. United Nations General Assembly Resolutions: A Six-Language Parallel Corpus. In *Proc. of the MT Summit XII*, pages 292–299, Ottawa.

S.Virpioja, J.J. Väyrynen, M. Creutz, and M. Sadeniemi. 2007. Morphology-aware statistical machine translation based on morphs induced in an unsupervised manner. In *Machine Translation Summit XI*, pages 491–498.

K. Toutanova, H. Suzuki, and A. Ruopp. 2008. Applying morphology generation models to machine translation. In *Proc. of the conference of the Association for Computational Linguistics and Human Language Technology (ACL-HLT)*, pages 514–522, Columbus, Ohio.

N. Ueffing and H. Ney. 2003. Using pos information for statistical machine translation into morphologically rich languages. In *Proc. of the 10th conference on European chapter of the Association for Computational Linguistics (EACL)*, pages 347–354, Stroudsburg, PA, USA.

# Baidu Translate: Research and Products

**Zhongjun HE**
Baidu Inc.
No. 10, Shangdi 10th Street, Beijing, 100085, China
hezhongjun@baidu.com

## 1 Overview

In this presentation, I would like to introduce the research and products of machine translation in Baidu. As the biggest Chinese search engine, Baidu has released its machine translation system in June, 2011. It now supports translations among 27 languages on multiple platforms, including PC, mobile devices, etc.

Hybrid translation approach is important for building an Internet translation system. As we know, the translation demands on the Internet come from various domains, including news wires, patents, poems, idioms, etc. It is difficult for a single translation system to achieve high accuracy on all domains. Therefore, hybrid translation is practically needed. Generally, we build a statistical machine translation (SMT) system, using the training corpora automatically crawled from the web. For the translation of idioms (e.g. *"有志者，事竟成,where there is a will, there is a way"*), hot words/expressions (e.g. *"一带一路, One Belt and One Road "*), example-based translation methods are used. To improve the translation of date (e.g. *"2012年7月6日, July 6, 2012"*), numbers (e.g. *"三千五百万, thirty-five million*), etc, rule-based methods are used as pre-process.

To improve translation quality for the resource-poor language pairs, we used pivot-based methods. Wu and Wang (2007) proposed the triangulation method that combines the source-pivot and the pivot-target phrase tables to induce a source-target phrase table. To fill up the data gap between the source-pivot and pivot-target corpora, Wu and Wang (2009) employed a hybrid method combining RBMT and SMT systems. We also proposed a method to use a Markov random walk to discover implicit relations between phrases in the source and target languages (Zhu et al., 2013), thus to improve the coverage of phrase pairs. We utilized the co-occurrence frequency of source-target phrase pairs to estimate phrase translation probabilities (Zhu et al., 2014).

On May 20th this year, we have launched a neural machine translation (NMT) system for Chinese-English translation. The system conducts end-to-end translation with a source language encoder and a target language decoder. Both the encoder and decoder are recurrent neural networks. The strength of NMT lies in that it can learn semantic and structural translation information by taking global contexts into account. We further integrated the SMT and NMT system to improve translation quality.

We also released off-line translation packs for NMT system on mobile devices, providing translation services in case that the Internet is unavailable. So far as we know, this is the first NMT system supporting off-line translation on mobile devices.

We also investigate the problem of learning a machine translation model that can simultaneously translate sentences from one source language to multiple target languages (Dong et al., 2015). Our solution is inspired by the recently proposed neural machine translation model which generalizes machine translation as a sequence learning problem. We train a unified neural machine translation model under the multi-task learning framework where the encoder is shared across different language pairs and each target language has a separate decoder. This model gets faster and better convergence for both resource-rich and resource-poor language pairs under the multi-task learning framework.

Based on the above techniques, we have released translation products for multiple platforms, including web translation on PC, APP on mobile devices, as well as free API for the third-party developers. Our system now support translations among 27 languages, not only including many frequently-used foreign languages, but also



*Proceedings of the ACL 2015 Fourth Workshop on Hybrid Approaches to Translation (HyTra)*, pages 61–62,
Beijing, China, July 31, 2015. 

including the traditional Chinese poem and Chinese dialects, for example, Cantonese. In order to make people communicate conveniently in foreign countries, the Baidu Translate APP supports speech-to-speech translation, object translation, instance full-screen translation, image translation, etc. Object translation enables users to identify objects and translate them into both Chinese and English. For the users who cannot speak and write foreign languages, the APP allows image as the input. For example, if you aim the cellphone camera at a menu written in a language you do not know, the translation will be displayed on the screen. Furthermore, rich information related to the food will also be displayed, including the materials, the taste, etc.

## 2 Outline

1. Introduction
   - Brief Introduction of Baidu MT
2. Hybrid Translation
   - SMT, EBMT and RBMT
   - Pivot-based Method for Resource-Poor Languages
3. Neural Machine Translation System
   - RNN Encoder-Decoder
   - Multi-task Learning
4. Products
   - Web
   - App
   - API

## 3 About the Speakers

Zhongjun He is a senior researcher in machine translation at Baidu. He received his Ph.D. in 2008 from Institute of Computing Technology, Chinese Academy of Sciences (ICT, CAS). He has more than ten years of research and development experiences on statistical machine translation.

## References


Daxiang Dong, Hua Wu, Wei He, Dianhai Yu, and Haifeng Wang. 2015. Multi-task learning for multiple language translation. In *To appear in ACL 2015*, Beijing, China, July.

Hua Wu and Haifeng Wang. 2007. Pivot language approach for phrase-based statistical machine translation. In *Proceedings of the 45th Annual Meeting of the Association for Computational Linguistics*, pages 856–863.

Hua Wu and Haifeng Wang. 2009. Revisiting pivot language approach for machine translation. In *Proceedings of the 47th Annual Meeting of the Association for Computational Linguistics and the 4th IJCNLP of the AFNLP*, pages 154–162.

Xiaoning Zhu, Zhongjun He, Hua Wu, Haifeng Wang, Conghui Zhu, and Tiejun Zhao. 2013. Improving pivot-based statistical machine translation using random walk. In *Proceedings of the 2013 Conference on Empirical Methods in Natural Language Processing*, page 524534, Seattle, Washington, USA, October.

Xiaoning Zhu, Zhongjun He, Hua Wu, Conghui Zhu, Haifeng Wang, and Tiejun Zhao. 2014. Improving pivot-based statistical machine translation by pivoting the co-occurrence count of phrase pairs. In *Proceedings of the 2014 Conference on Empirical Methods in Natural Language Processing*, pages 1665–1675, Doha, Qatar, October.

**On Improving the Human Translation Process by Using MT Technologies under a Cognitive Framework**

Geng Xinhui
CTO of CCID TransTech
Beijing, China
gengxh@ccidtrans.com
http://www.ccidtrans.com/

The translation process is regarded as a complex cognitive process and one of the core topics in cognitive translatology. Unlike how machine translation post-editing works, which only needs a machine translation result, we divide the translation process into several cognitive subtasks and use the technology in MT to help the implementation of each subtask. We aim to make each subtask completed automatically or semi-automatically and evaluate the improvement of cognitive effort cost by adopting the cognitive measure approach. In this way, a cognitive framework is expected to be built for the use and development of MT technology.



*Proceedings of the ACL 2015 Fourth Workshop on Hybrid Approaches to Translation (HyTra)*, page 63,
Beijing, China, July 31, 2015. ©2015 Association for Computational Linguistics

## Towards a shared task for shallow semantics-based translation (in an industrial setting)

Kurt Eberle
CEO of Lingenio GmbH
Heidelberg, Germany
k.eberle@lingenio.de
http://www.lingenio.de/

In the Lingenio analysis systems, the sentences are analyzed into syntactic slot grammar representations from which so called 'dependency trees' are derived which reduce the analyses to the semantically relevant nodes and decorate these by information from the semantic lexicon. Slot grammar is a unification-based dependency grammar (cf. McCord 89). It has been used in the Logic based Machine Translation project (LMT) of IBM and underlies the commercial (rule-based) MT systems that developed from this project as spin-off: Personal Translator (linguatec Sprachtechnologien GmbH), translate (Lingenio GmbH) and the (rule-based) systems of Synthema. IBM uses slot grammar for deep analysis in IBM's Watson.



*Proceedings of the ACL 2015 Fourth Workshop on Hybrid Approaches to Translation (HyTra)*, page 64,
Beijing, China, July 31, 2015. ©2015 Association for Computational Linguistics

# Author Index